FOR GOD AND NEIGHBOUR

Padre Pio blessing the author Anthony Pandiscia

Anthony Pandiscia

FOR GOD
AND NEIGHBOUR

The life and work of Padre Pio

St Paul Publications

Original Title: *Un contadino cerca Dio: Padre Pio*
© 1990 Edizioni Paoline s.r.l., Cinisello Balsamo (Milano), Italy

Translated by Susan Leslie

St Paul Publications
Middlegreen, Slough SL3 6BT, United Kingdom

English translation copyright © St Paul Publications, UK 1991

ISBN 085439 373 0

Printed by The Guernsey Press Co. Guernsey, C.I.

St Paul Publications is an activity of the priests and brothers of the Society
of St Paul who proclaim the Gospel through the media of social communication

Contents

PART 2: TESTIMONIES

APPENDIX:

Foreword

My first memories of Padre Pio go back to my boyhood days. Then my sister and I had to walk twelve miles with our mother to make our confession to him. He was amiable and kind and never failed to ask after our family. And despite so many demands on him, Padre Pio always found time to encourage me in my studies for the priesthood and later in my work as a Comboni missionary in Africa. He was truly my spiritual director, confessor and guardian angel.

Indeed, Padre Pio's friendship with our family also meant working a discreet miracle or two. He was kind, reassuring and protective towards my mother. In 1926 when communication was difficult, Padre Pio foretold, two months before the event, the death of my father in a mining accident in the States, and our family found a veritable source of strength and comfort in Padre Pio.

At another time, when I was in Africa, rumours spread in our village that I had been devoured by a lion. My mother rushed to Padre Pio, who roared with laughter as he said to her: 'Run along, run along now. Your little Peter is more alive and kicking than you are!'

Then there was the case of my mother's own illness. Cancer. Doctors in Rome had given her two weeks. But she lived for another seven years, and when she died, it was not of cancer. It was a miracle. And I knew who had done it. When I went to see Padre Pio, he said: 'Well, I saw how terrible you looked, and your sister was even worse. . . Well . . . Well, then . . . ,' he continued, slapping my shoulder in a gesture of affection, 'let the Lord be praised.'

Antonio Pandiscia's book, which I have read, rather devoured, with true religious devotion and tender affection, is more than a lively, honest and accurate biography. It is such a genuine and fascinating portrait that those who, like me, have been privileged from their young days to know Padre Pio are certain to derive from the book the feeling of seeing, hearing and touching him again. Reading the book, I relived my numerous meetings with him in his humble (famous) cell no. 5. It made me recall, after twenty-seven years, his gentle and affectionate words in reply to my request for his prayers. Showing me the wounds of the stigmata in his hands, he said: 'Peter, when I place someone in here you can be sure that they are never forgotten.'

The publishers of the English edition of Pandiscia's book have done well to give it the title *For God and Neighbour*. It is difficult to think of a more comprehensive or precise way of summing up the life and suffering of this man consumed by the love of his God and fellow beings. Everyone had access to Padre Pio. There was never any distinction of age, gender or social status. He was brother and father to all. 'When you miss your father, mother, brother, sister, nephew, niece, or friend,' Padre Pio used to say to us, 'come to me.' But in him we also found God.

We found God in Padre Pio because he was a man of prayer. He was, like our best-loved St Francis of Assisi himself, 'man made prayer'. His long days (sometimes eighteen hours in the confessional) were totally immersed in prayer. His advice for making the world a better place was: 'Pray and help those who suffer. Pray for peace in the world. Pray always.'

To prayer was added another dimension. Suffering. If the life of Jesus was a 'cross of suffering', then it could not have been otherwise for one who has been described as the perfect copy of Jesus crucified. Even in visible signs — there were others — Jesus wished his disciple to be like himself. The wounds of the pierced heart, hands and feet were but the exterior marks of that interior martyrdom of suffering in which Padre Pio rejoiced.

For all the inconveniences, misunderstandings and sufferings caused by his stigmata, Padre Pio was no sniveller or sulker. On the contrary, he radiated a joy that was irrepressible. 'The happiness I experience,' he said to us one day, 'is so extreme that I want to share it with others who in turn will help me to thank the Lord.'

In this foreword I have been able to bear personal witness to our beloved Padre Pio. Let me therefore conclude with an independent testimony. This is what Frank Killbride of Yorkshire television said to me about Padre Pio: 'This is his quality: compassion, joy and laughter. I was telling David Frost, the famous television interviewer, that no one could speak of Padre Pio without smiling. If that isn't the finest tribute to any person, I don't know what is.'

Peter Villani
Comboni Missionaries, London

Part 1

THE LIFE AND WORK
OF PADRE PIO

Chapter 1

The 'non-confession'

'How long is it since you last went to confession?' he asked me as I knelt down.

'A couple of months, Father.'

'How long is it since you last went to confession?'

'About two months, Father.'

'How long is it since you last went to confession?' he asked again, almost angrily.

'Father, I don't really remember but not many months ago.'

'Be off with you, liar, heretic, that's what you are. It's been months and months since you last asked God's forgiveness.'

That was my first, brief confession to Padre Pio. I was deeply disturbed by his harsh words and disapproving look. Disconcerted, I struggled to my feet. It did not seem possible to go on with my confession like this. I would have liked to receive absolution, I had gone there for that; but I understood that perhaps I did not deserve it. His words had hurt me so much that they aroused in me a deep sense of guilt.

After some time I returned to the village of San Giovanni Rotondo in the province of Foggia, in southern Italy, still with the intention of making my confession or rather trying to do so. With my heart in my mouth, I approached the confessional. As I knelt down and made the sign of the cross Padre Pio said suddenly:

'How long is it since you last went to Holy Mass?'

'I go every Sunday, Father.'

'How long have you not been going to Mass?' he insisted.

'Well, Father, sometimes I don't go to Mass on Sundays through pressure of work,' I answered, knowing very well, after my previous experience, that it was no good tampering with the truth. In this way I hoped to win his sympathy. Instead, this is what I heard:

'Be off with you, nasty liar and heretic! So you find time for amusements but not for the Lord?'

I rose with lowered eyes. I felt humiliated by this fresh rebuff and I went slowly away, knowing in my heart that I would never receive absolution from Padre Pio if I went on coming to him with approximations to the truth and without the necessary spiritual preparation. Nor was I reassured by the fact that other penitents, too, for various reasons, had been summarily dismissed by the friar.

I decided to stay in San Giovanni Rotondo in order to make serious preparations for my confession to Padre Pio.

After a few days I finally felt ready but when my turn came, I hesitated for a few moments wondering whether to go and kneel before the friar and confess my sins or to wait a little longer. But Padre Pio's voice rang out:

'Come on, lad, will you hurry up? You're wasting my time!'

Taken aback, I hastily knelt down at his feet.

'What, didn't you want to confess any more?'

'No, Father, I was just afraid of the kind of reception I might get from you.'

'I'm hardly the master of the house!' he answered, starting to smile. Then he added: 'And you wanted to go away, just now when you're better prepared than the other times to approach the Lord?'

I confessed my sins very freely as if I were talking to a friend and received absolution. I went out of the church feeling lighter, as if a great weight had rolled off me.

Chapter 2

The meeting

I was still very young when my parents took me for the first time to see Padre Pio. I was maybe ten or eleven years old and I really wanted to meet the friar of San Giovanni because he was often mentioned at home and it was said that he worked miracles and had the stigmata like Jesus.

From Foggia, where we lived, we went to San Giovanni Rotondo by way of a long white road, very dusty and full of stones. I remember that as we climbed up towards the Friary of Our Lady of Grace my father said to me:

'You'll soon be seeing the friar with the stigmata. You'll be meeting Padre Pio, the holy friar.'

'But if he has the stigmata does it mean that he's like Jesus?' I asked curiously.

'Yes, that's right, he's like Jesus. And he suffers like Jesus.'

It was springtime, probably the month of April: I remember I had no overcoat, I was wearing a pullover. And it was afternoon. Perhaps he had already finished hearing confessions.

I met him in the old friary chapel in front of the confessional; I knelt down like the others and kissed his hand, he put his hand on my head and talked to my father. I don't remember what they said, maybe I did not even hear; I was moved and a little afraid in the presence of such a famous and unusual person. I remember staring at his hands which gave off an acrid and penetrating odour and I thought I should see the stigmata but instead they were covered by wool mittens. Although everyone knew about the stigmata and he had endured many humiliating official examinations of them, Padre Pio kept them carefully concealed. By that time he had been wearing his wool mittens, winter and summer, for many years.

I heard him say so while he was talking to my parents.

The whole thing was not very clear to me but I accepted it. For me Padre Pio was none other than Jesus and when I went home I told my younger brothers and sisters that I had actually met Jesus, who wore mittens, which aroused their curiosity and envy.

I remember that on the way back from San Giovanni Rotondo I felt lighthearted and happy. Certainly all children feel like that after an outing but I felt as if I'd been to some great celebration, as if I'd had a pleasant afternoon's entertainment. For a long time afterwards I remembered that meeting with great pleasure and happiness. It was 1948. Italy was still suffering from the devastation of the last war. San Giovanni Rotondo was a forgotten village and in order to get there one had to 'entrust one's soul to God.' But the name of Padre Pio was already known.

Chapter 3

The future Padre Pio

Francesco Forgione was born in Pietrelcina in the province of Benevento in the Neapolitan region on 25 May 1887. The following day at six o'clock in the morning he was baptized in the Church of Sant'Anna which stands a few yards from his house.

Only thirteen hours had gone by since his coming into the world and his father Grazio, a very devout peasant, lost no time for fear the child should die before being baptized. His fear was not unfounded. At that time infant mortality was very high and Grazio and his wife Maria Giuseppa had already lost two children: Francesco who died after nineteen days and Amelia who had lived just twenty months. Only Michele, who was then five years old, had survived (they were to have four more children). But little Francesco, who had inherited the name of their first-born, was in no danger although his health would always be delicate.

The house where the future Padre Pio was born was divided into two sections, two tiny rooms with no communicating door. To get from the kitchen area to the sleeping quarters, you had to go out into the street. It was a poor dwelling, or rather just a passage furnished with a truckle bed, a metal basin, two straw-bottomed chairs, a shabby sideboard of red wood and a large container in which flour was kept for the winter. Both parents were illiterate. All they could offer to their newborn son was a primitive wooden cradle, painted red.

At night the plump little Francesco was very restless in his cradle and sometimes he even upset it. One can easily picture the parents' anxiety as they got out of bed and rushed to pick him up, fearing he had hurt himself. Instead they always found him smiling as if he were pleased to have woken Mum and Dad!

As a small boy Francesco was restless and so naughty that

7

his father Grazio had to punish him and sometimes even to smack him until finally, in desperation at the young rascal's pranks, he stopped sending him to pasture the sheep and left him instead in the care of a little friend who was older than him, Baldino Vecchiarino by name. Francesco was barely six years old at the time!

It was in fact Baldino who later told how he had seen Francesco draw the sign of the cross on the ground and remain kneeling there for some time in prayer, heedless of his friend who was calling him and shaking him hard. Poor Baldino, much struck by the odd behaviour of his companion, ran home in fear and told his parents all about it but they did not believe him.

The same thing happened often and one morning Francesco, noticing that his friend was looking at him strangely, asked: 'Why are you looking at me in that odd way? Why don't you pray with me?' The good Baldino, shaken by these words, looked at the ground and answered, 'But when you pray it's as if you were dead and no longer in this world!'

However, after that day Baldino sometimes joined in his friend's prayers for a while, going on as long as he could. For hours on end, in fact, Francesco would stretch himself out on the bare earth, gazing at the sky, daydreaming or maybe thinking who knows what? His moods varied: sometimes he was completely carefree and elated, sometimes extremely sad; when his face darkened, he looked the picture of gloom. This began to happen frequently and it worried his poor parents who unfortunately did not have too much time to devote to him as they also had to look after the other children and provide for the needs of their large family.

When they decided to send him to school to join the local infants' class, his teacher Mandato Sagittario made enormous efforts to teach him writing and arithmetic. Sometimes Francesco Forgione's exercise book was full of crosses rather than penstrokes. With a second teacher, Angelo Caccamo, he succeeded in passing his elementary examinations.

Apart from these few details, we have very little information about Padre Pio's childhood. We know that for several years his father was in America searching for the good life which a small country village could not offer. But, as Maria Winowska writes in her book *The real face of Padre Pio*, '. . . he was born in a village with fine traditions of Christianity and humanity, where the spirits of the people are as effervescent as the hill wines, a breed honed by centuries of austere virtue, a people who joyfully bring forth masterpieces.' Masterpieces of humanity and holiness.

At Morcone in the province of Benevento, he went to the high school and entered the local Capuchin friary on 6 January 1903.

The Catholic writer Luigi Tucci, a spiritual son of Padre Pio, notes in his book *A sign of Providence*: 'By the time his boyhood was nearly over and already the things of God had began to exercise a deep fascination over him, a fascination which was soon to become irresistible. Meanwhile, his mind was concentrated on the only goal which brings peace to the soul. Silently and tenaciously he set himself to persevere in his vocation.'

At the age of fifteen Francesco turned his back definitively on the world and its illusory values and prepared himself for the life of a Capuchin. It was in 1902, on 20 January, that this calm and happy fifteen-year-old, already knowing what he wanted in life, took his first steps in his chosen calling. No hardship troubled him at that moment: neither winter cold nor community life, nor leaving his home. He was now Fra Pio of Pietrelcina, having taken the name of his native village as both heritage and device as he started his life of betrothal to Lady Poverty.

Morcone is a small village where the peasants still rise at daybreak to cultivate the fields which yield the coarse black country bread. It is the place which represents not only an important stage in Padre Pio's life but also something of fundamental value to him. He will often remember Morcone and cell number 78 where he first undertook to suffer for the Lord and where he received the habit. The door of this cell still bears the motto: 'Without much care and diligence you will never acquire virtue.'

It was in the friary of Morcone that he received the Capuchin habit on 22 January 1903, before the father provincial, Pio da Benevento. He was sure now that he would dedicate his whole life to the Lord. It was in the small friary at Morcone that Fra Pio decided to offer his life for the good of humanity, seeking in prayer the true succour for the woes of the world.

Fra Pio spent his days in complete solitude, meeting his brothers at the Liturgical Hours, in the refectory for the frugal meals, generously supplied by the local peasants, and during walks in the courtyard. But while the others held animated conversations, played games and generally amused themselves, he was far away in spirit, his lips always moving in prayer, his face absorbed in profound meditation; even if he was in company, he did not stop praying. In the end his companions came to understand this and left him in peace. At night in cell 78 they would see a flickering paraffin light, sole companion of the lonely friar from Pietrelcina who spent a good part of the night in praising God.

A school composition by Padre Pio

The strange dream of a shepherd boy.

Fernando was a poor shepherd boy who was thinking of becoming a friar; but his parents were poor and could not help him to do this. While he was sleeping one night, he dreamed that he was in the monastery, already dressed as a friar.

It seemed to him that it was the first day he had been there and after the meal in the refectory he went down into the garden with the other novices, accompanied by the novice master.

Then, with the permission of that superior, they started to play ball, water the flowers, dig the little garden; in fact they were all doing something and none of them stood idle.

After about two hours of such occupations, the bell rang for Vespers and the shepherd boy friar had to go to the church where the sound of the organ and the chanting of the holy psalms filled his heart with immense joy. How happy he was! His wish had finally been granted! But it was a dream and sadly he realized it when he awoke because he was in his little bed as on the previous night while his heart was still overflowing with joy.

How bitter was his disappointment!

The poor little boy still had to care for his flock, enjoying the songs of various birds, but he could not lend his ear to the beautiful mystical sound of the church organ and the sweet chanting of holy psalms!

Pietrelcina, August 1902

Francesco Forgione

A glimpse of the future

Padre Pio's fundamental attitude, his mystical spirituality, his rock-like faith, his love for the suffering, all came together in a vision of the future which he had at the end of 1902 and of which he spoke in the third person to his confessor:

'Francesco saw at his side a man of rare beauty, shining like the sun, who invited him to follow him and to fight valiantly. Before Francesco's eyes there stretched an immense plain with two groups of men on it: one group consisted of many men dressed in white with beautiful faces, the other of as many dressed in black with repulsive faces. Between them strode a fearsome individual, so tall that his forehead touched the clouds. The resplendent man promised to give Francesco his entire support if he would fight the monstrous men. The encounter was terrible but in the end Francesco prevailed and all the vile men fled. As a reward Francesco won a splendid crown and the promise of another, incomparably beautiful, if he would spend his whole life fighting the vile men.'

That is a brief and succinct summary of Padre Pio's life, his unrelenting struggle against the forces of evil, his building up of a kingdom of God through prayer and his constant contact with suffering humanity.

Chapter 4

The novitiate

From the Morcone friary, Fra Pio went to that of Sant'Elia in Pianisi a few miles away where he stayed from 2 February 1904 until 15 November 1906. In this new house of prayer he studied philosophy and prepared for the priesthood. While at Sant'Elia, Fra Pio first heard of San Giovanni Rotondo where it was announced that a new Capuchin friary was to open on the south Italian tableland of Gargano. Among his confrères there was one young man particularly interested in the new foundation because, being from that area himself, he wished to be transferred so as to be nearer his family. Fra Pio said to him, 'I will be assigned to San Giovanni Rotondo not long after the friary opens.' He only meant it as a joke but these proved to be prophetic words. The Friary of Our Lady of Grace was opened in 1909 and a few years later Padre Pio, as he was then, joined it as spiritual director. First, however, he moved several times. From the Friary of Saint'Elia in Pianisi which was in need of restoration, he was transferred to San Marco La Catola, in the province of Foggia. It was his first contact with the district of Puglia which was to revere him as 'the man who knocks at God's door.' After that he was transferred to Serracapriola, still in the province of Foggia, where he continued his theological studies.

Meanwhile, he started to show signs of fatigue: his face would suddenly flush and then go deathly pale, which made him both physically weak and depressed. Also, he began to eat less and less food, of poorer quality. Only his community spirit made him join his brothers at mealtimes. His many hours of study alternated with those of prayer which were always long and interminable. This was a real need of his soul, a spiritual necessity felt, but his youthful physique could not take the heavy strain. One night in July 1907 a confrère heard feeble cries coming from Fra Pio's cell. He ran along anxiously to find him face down on the floor, his eyes staring and his breath coming in gasps. So his superiors decided to send him for a while to his home village of Pietrelcina in the hope that his native air would do him good. Fra Pio spent a few months at home and it seems that staying in his parents' house was beneficial. He began to smile again and made jokes at times. He took long walks across the fields where he had once been a shepherd; as in the past, he gazed at the sky and the stars, daydreaming: he became a simple child again as when he used to pasture the flock with his friend Baldino.

At the end of the year he returned to Serracapriola where he stayed until February 1908. He was then transferred to the friary of Montefusco in the province of Avellino for two years. While there, he completed his theological studies and received minor orders.

In the green Neapolitan countryside of Irpinia, in the silence of the woods and living among kindly people, Fra Pio spent his time acquiring an even deeper grasp of spiritual matters. The local inhabitants would see him go by, rosary in hand, and greet him, but mostly they received no answer; the young friar was too absorbed in God. One day a youth, annoyed by the lack of response to his greeting, came up to him and asked him irritably why he adopted such an anti-social attitude. Fra Pio smiled and asked him:

'Do you pray to Our Lady?'

'Yes,' replied the young man.

'Well then, let me give my time to the Mother of God, too.'

The last stage of his priestly formation ended on 10 August 1910 in Benevento Cathedral with his ordination to the priesthood. Luigi Tucci, one of his spiritual sons who witnessed the ceremony, writes:

'Here he is, on the threshold of the cathedral on 10 August 1910, ready to put on the gold ring of Lady Poverty and to receive in return the priestly diadem and the power to be a fisher of men. The fulfilment of another dream arouses unspeakable joy in Fra Pio's heart and he seems to shake like a blade of grass in the wind. All is ready to go forward in a spirit of joy. The bells ring out in festal tones. His mother Giuseppa, who has come on foot from Pietrelcina, has already taken her seat in the cathedral with tears of joy in her eyes. "Uncle Grazio" is absent but gives his son his blessing from far-off America. The very air seems to be scented, full of solemnity and majesty. Pale and tense with emotion, his eyes burning, he walks awkwardly towards the altar, then prostrates himself humbly on the bare stone and remains there for a long time, his heart scarcely beating in his breast. Thus it is that the former novice receives the priestly chrism. Still humble and recollected, the new priest takes leave of us calmly; but we can already sense his new role, already we seem to see, in a blaze of light, the spiritual giant, the "Padre" who will one day climb Gargano to draw multitudes of men and women into the way of God. Then mother and son set off once more for Pietrelcina where the new priest will celebrate his first Mass, the morning after the ordination.'

On his return to Morcone, his state of health was still poor: very high fevers would alternate with very low temperatures; his face was extremely pale. Again his superiors thought of sending him to Pietrelcina for a time of rest.

Chapter 5

Apparitions

It was during his stay in Pietrelcina that Fra Pio became aware of special divine protection.

He suffered physically and spiritually, being subject to diabolical temptations and then he would receive marvellous consolations from Jesus: at first, only in the form of voices; later there were actual apparitions.

Fra Pio accepted these, not as exceptionl happenings but as normal events in the spiritual life: he accepted them without question, so deep was his faith. He spoke of them in letters to Father Benedetto da San Marco in Lamis, his spiritual director, and to his confessor, Father Agostino da San Marco in Lamis, asking them to destroy this information after having read it and not to show it to others. Fortunately for us, this request was not granted, so we can read the actual letters which are so human and simple yet dramatic and full of depth and vitality. They reveal a different side of Padre Pio: gentle, timid, very human. Here is an example, addressed to Father Agostino, dated 16 March 1912:

Dear Father,

I am constantly being overwhelmed by divine consolation. At times I feel this excessive sweetness is going to kill me and I am on the point of saying to Jesus as St Augustine did, 'Ah, Lord, I wish I could die so that I could see you.' But that moment has not yet come, Father.

Meanwhile the devil would like to destroy me. But long live Jesus! May the Lord give you joy both in this world and the next for all you have done on my behalf with Father Provincial.

Goodbye, dear Father,
Most affectionately,
Your poor disciple,
Fra Pio

There were trials and diabolical temptations as well as

misunderstanding and persecution on the part of men, but at the same time he was beginning to have personal conversations with Jesus, spiritual and mystical dialogues which took place usually after his morning communion:

'Every morning he comes to me and pours his love and goodness into my heart.

If I could, I would wish with my blood those places where I have scandalized so many souls.

But praised be the constant mercy of Jesus, who asks me for love. And my heart more than my mouth answers him, "Oh my Jesus, I would like to . . ." and then I cannot go on. But in the end I exclaim, "Yes, Jesus, I love you at this moment . . . and I also feel the need to love you more; but Jesus, if you want more love, take this heart of mine and fill it with your own love and then command me to love you too; which I won't refuse to do; I ask you to do it, I desire it." '

So runs an extract from the letter of 1 March 1912, also addressed to Father Agostino. In the same letter, Fra Pio turns to the subject of the pain he feels every week from Tuesday to Saturday:

'From Thursday evening until Saturday, and also on Tuesdays, I am in an agony of pain. My heart, hands and feet seem to be transfixed by a sword, the pain is so great.'

Those were days of anguish for Padre Pio; his life was by that time a succession of visits by mysterious persons, physical torments, endless temptations and wonderful moments of conversation with Jesus.

'On Friday morning I was still in bed when Jesus appeared to me. He was wretched and disfigured. He showed me a great crowd of religious and secular priests and several church dignitaries. Some of them were celebrating Mass, some in the act of putting on, some taking off the sacred vestments. I was much grieved to see Jesus in anguish so I asked him why he was suffering so much. I received no answer from him. But he looked at the priests and then, as if he were tired of looking at them, averted his gaze and when he looked up again at me, I saw to my horror that tears were running down his cheeks. He walked away from the crowd of priests with a look of deep disgust and loathing, shouting, "Butchers!" Turning to me, he said, "My son, don't think

16

my agony lasted for three hours, no, I shall be in agony until the end of the world on account of those souls whom I have blessed most richly. You mustn't sleep while I am in agony, my son. My soul goes in search of a few signs of human sympathy but alas, they don't care and they leave me alone. My agony is increased by the ingratitude and spiritual somnolence of my ministers. Alas, how poorly they respond to my love. What hurts me most is that they're unbelieving and contemptuous as well as indifferent."

Jesus said more, but I could never tell anyone in this world what he said.'

He speaks of another vision in a letter of 7 July 1913. Jesus appeared to him suddenly after Mass. Fra Pio gives this account of Christ's words:

'My son, be sure to write down what you hear me say today so that you don't forget it. I am faithful. No one will be lost unless he so chooses. Light is very different from darkness. When I wish to speak to a soul, I draw it constantly towards me; the devil, on the other hand, tends to lure souls away from me.

At certain times in their lives, people fear for their eternal salvation. They may rest assured: if their fear is followed by peace and serenity, it is a fear inspired by me.'

Chapter 6

Padre Pio and confession

I have always counted myself very fortunate that I was able to have more contact with Padre Pio than most people. My family comes from Lacedonia in the province of Avellino next to Naples but at the end of 1940 we went to live, first at Ascoli Satriano and then, in 1948, at Foggia because my father's job as a tax-collector took him to that region. There he was very friendly with the superior of the Sant'Anna friary, which founded San Giovanni Rotondo. A devout Catholic, my father used to see a lot of the Capuchin friars at Foggia and then at San Giovanni, and Padre Pio was among them. As I grew up, I formed similar bonds of friendship and familiarity with the friars. I made friends with many of them, above all with Padre Lino da Prato, superior of the Sant'Anna friary at Foggia and, thanks to this friendship, each time I decided to go to San Giovanni, even if I went on the spur of the moment, I was able to go into the friary and see or talk to Padre Pio.

All my meetings with him meant a lot to me; they were times of great peace. It is enough to look at the photographs we had taken of us together: he looks relaxed and smiling. Once he told me a joke. I was still a university student and he asked me:

'What do you want to do with your life?'

'I'm doing a law degree and I'd like to be a journalist as well as a lawyer.'

'Ah, what a fine profession,' he replied sarcastically. 'Listen to this little story: One day all the lawyers got together in heaven and realized that they hadn't got a patron saint. They went to St Peter and told him about this. St Peter acknowledged their complaint and suggested, "Let's put a blindfold on one of you and lead him round heaven and the first saint he touches shall be your patron." This proposal was accepted, the blindfolded lawyer went round heaven and at a certain moment he bumped into something;

18

he stopped, took off the blindfold and saw that he had touched the tail of St Michael's dragon. From then on, St Michael's dragon has been the patron of lawyers.'

Padre Pio told me this simple joke, which was more ironical than malicious, to make fun of me. He often made fun of lawyers and journalists; 'journalist' for him was synonymous with 'liar'. I never had any difficulty relating to him although his penetrating gaze sometimes made me lower my eyes with a kind of reverential fear. But I was not the only one. I have often noticed the same reaction in many other Catholics. When he came on the scene, he had such a majestic presence that everyone else seemed to get smaller. The stigmatic friar always listened in a fatherly way to those who crowded round him seeking a word of comfort, a prayer or a blessing. He did treat some of them badly and could be extremely brusque but Padre Pio's every word and gesture bore witness to his mystical and human understanding of sinners. He loved humanity, his constant prayer was for others, his sufferings were offered continually for the good of other human beings.

One day I crept up to the balustrade of the central aisle of the Church of Our Lady of Grace, the place where Padre Pio used to retire to pray and, kneeling down near him, I awaited his blessing. The minutes went by slowly but the friar did not seem to notice me. I reached out to touch him and instead of a blessing I received a sharp reproof: 'What are you doing here? Why are you disturbing someone who is praying?'

Embarrassed, I answered, 'Father, I found the door open and I just had to come and greet you.'

He said even more distantly, 'First learn to make the sign of the cross in the Lord's house and then greet people.'

'But Father, I did make the sign of the cross . . .'

'Don't tell fibs, you came in brushing your forehead and your nose . . .'

'Yes, it's true, I crossed myself in a hurry,' I admitted, 'but only out of anxiety to see you.'

'You young people don't know how to pray. Yet humanity has such need of our prayers!'

Nothing escaped Padre Pio. His searching glance could disquiet both the faithful and the penitent. At first it was just terribly embarrassing. Later on it sometimes reduced one to tears.

Like a powerful magnet, Padre Pio's confessional drew thousands of people from all over Italy and from abroad; this meant very long hours spent in counselling penitents, which exhausted him. To confess to him was to touch new depths of self-awareness and truth but it could also be disturbing as he was very demanding.

Sinners who sought the consolation of Padre Pio's absolution were not permitted to make excuses or to justify themselves. Perhaps this severe attitude raised questions in some minds about the whole concept of forgiveness which is the main object of confession; but it was no good going to the friar of San Giovanni without absolute sincerity in confessing one's sins and a true purpose of amendment. Padre Pio believed that the sinner should be aware of his sin and should not try to diminish its importance in the eyes of the confessor by pleading extenuating circumstances. My father went to confession to him and eventually mentioned his problems with us, his children. 'You mustn't spare the rod if you're going to be a good father,' advised Padre Pio.

Padre Pio, as I have said, could see into everyone's soul. This legendary ability of his was the most disconcerting to those who came to him intending to hide some serious matter and so failing to make a clean breast of their sins. Only in such cases was he harsh and fearful in his rebukes; he saw that such penitents had come without a true desire to be relieved of their burden. Unfortunately, I myself was sometimes among such careless and uncommitted Christians!

Confession to Padre Pio was a brief affair. A thin cotton curtain in a draughty corner of the sacristy was all the privacy accorded to the penitent. Then, face to face with the saint of Gargano, sinners would find themselves as it were naked and ill at ease, their worldliness mercilessly exposed; as the friar made his scorching comments, spiritual values seemed suddenly to assume gigantic proportions. I confessed to Padre Pio on several occasions and at least half of those times I was sent away, either because I was not completely sincere or because I lacked humility in seeking forgiveness or because I was not truly repentant of the sins which I continued to commit. And each time I drew aside

20

the confessional curtain and went back to my everyday life, my very soul felt seared by his words. I could have avoided these encounters or gone to another confessor but his attraction was too strong for me.

However, when people received his absolution, you could see by their happy faces and eyes that they had been freed from the burden of their sins and many bore witness to feelings of exceptional spiritual well-being. They felt closer to God and further from the petty concerns of this world. They almost felt like running . . . running towards the new light which the friar had kindled in their hearts. This explains why, every day, the faithful could be found in their hundreds patiently awaiting their moment of truth, apprehensive at the thought of facing the stigmatic friar who was severe with sinners, liars and the indecisive, but gentle with those who opened their hearts to him, eager for a word of comfort.

So many men and women came to Padre Pio's confessional that it became necessary to set up a proper office to regulate the flow of penitents, and the order in which they were seen. This order was strictly observed, regardless of the distance from which penitents had come; it did not matter if they were ordinary folk, bishops or ministers . . . or even crowned heads!

At the beginning of 1946, Queen Maria José came incognito to San Giovanni Rotondo to meet the stigmatic friar. There were two ladies-in-waiting with her. The brothers of the little friary were quite overwhelmed when they saw their illustrious visitor and hastened to do her bidding. The father guardian went in search of Padre Pio and found him in the confessional. They told him about his unusual visitor but Padre Pio asked him to go away because he was hearing the confession of a poor woman of the people. Maria José could wait. This attitude seemed quite normal to him but not everybody approved of his having kept the queen waiting and it evidently earned him a reproof as, a few days later, he felt duty bound to write to his superior in Foggia:

San Giovanni Rotondo, February 1946

My dear Father,
May Jesus be with you always and guide you in your mission.
 I humbly ask your pardon if I kept the Queen Maria José

waiting but there was an ordinary woman ahead of her in the queue, a poor miller's wife who sometimes comes to me for confession, leaving her young children in the care of a neighbour. And she always feels very anxious about these innocent souls at home, waiting from moment to moment for their mother to return. It's true they are both mothers, both have their troubles, but I could not leave one mother to go running to the other. Both of them had come to the Lord and the good Jesus opens his arms to all, including those who are waiting and know how to wait!

Please forgive me for what I have done and I will pray the Lord to give me strength to overcome my faults.

Yours,

Padre Pio

He asked pardon but was probably convinced that he had done the right thing. The miller's children took precedence because they were more needy than the queen.

He loved children: he saw in them a pure outlook on life, innocence, blessedness. When a child came up to him, he would smile and caress it and if some babe in arms pulled his beard, Padre Pio would let it go on playing. He really had a weakness for children. He would have done anything to see them smiling and happy. To him they represented the best and most hopeful aspect of humanity. It was of them that Jesus had said, 'Let the little ones come to me.'

At one time, a well-known Roman journalist, a colleague of mine, had a daughter who had to have a serious operation. Knowing that I used to visit Padre Pio, my friend asked me to go to San Giovanni Rotondo and ask his prayers for the child's healing. I arrived at the friary in the morning while Padre Pio was celebrating Mass. I waited until he had finished and when I went up to kiss his hand I found him suddenly brusque and severe. He frowned at me and said, 'What do you want from me that you come looking for me? I can't do anything, I can't do anything.'

'I only came to say "hello" and hear Mass.'

'That's not true, but I can't do anything. Besides, they need children, they need little angels in heaven.' So I realized that he had seen and understood everything. Without me having told him, he knew why I had come. I had got my friend to give me a photograph of the little girl; I showed it to him.

'Padre Pio,' I said, 'but how . . . this beautiful child . . . look! What does it matter if they need angels in heaven? The parents are desperate.'

But he just repeated: 'I can't do anything about it, I can't do a thing,' as if he were talking to himself. I insisted, I begged him; for a moment he was about to throw me out and would have done so if he had not understood that my insistence was due to the deep misery I felt, for I realized that his attitude meant that the child was going to die. In the end, seeing there was nothing to be done, I resigned myself and asked him if he could at least send a short message of comfort to the parents. He gave me part of his rosary saying, 'Take that to them and tell them to pray to Our Lady for the child.' A few days later after the operation, the little girl died.

That was the only time I left San Giovanni Rotondo feeling resentful towards the friar who had not answered my prayer.

Chapter 7

San Giovanni Rotondo

San Giovanni Rotondo is a rough and stony village on the slopes of Mount Gargano, the spur of Italy which separates the plateau of Puglia from the Adriatic Sea. Forgotten for centuries, it was the sort of village where, until recently, the people kept their family's sole assets, their mules and asses, indoors, thus protecting them from bad weather or theft. Nowadays the village flourishes in the hard mountainous country as an oasis of hope and healing for those who are sick in body or soul. It was a miraculous transformation and it has a name: Padre Pio da Pietrelcina.

It was on 28 July 1916 that Father Agostino da San Marco in Lamis first went to San Giovanni Rotondo with Padre Pio.

The streets of the forgotten village of Gargano were cobbled. Access to the newly re-opened Friary of Our Lady of Grace was by a two-kilometre footpath through the countryside. The friars went on foot: Padre Pio was panting and sweating but hardly had he reached the humble rustic dwelling when his face lit up. He was strongly drawn to this wild country and the deep stillness made him feel close to God. But that was only a fleeting visit to the Gargano friary. He then went back to Foggia to the Sant'Anna friary where he had been sent. It cost him some pain to leave San Giovanni Rotondo and he missed it badly. But obedience is one of the main rules of his order. However, hardly had he arrived in Foggia when he asked his superior to send him to the friary at San Giovanni Rotondo. His request was granted. In this way the lighthearted prophecy he had made to his confrère at Sant'Elia was to be fulfilled.

From then on, the Gargano area was 'all his', entrusted to his ministry. Padre Pio was happy to live on this rocky mountain. In a letter to his parents he wrote:

My dearest parents,

After a tiring journey, I arrived in my domain of San Giovanni Rotondo. The good Father Agostino da San Marco in Lamis came with me and during the journey we asked the Lord several times to give us strength to minister to suffering souls. There are two brothers with me at the friary, Paolino and Nicola. We have already recited three rosaries together to Our Lady. I feel I am going to be here for a very long time and never leave. It's a great day for me, although I feel much oppressed in my spirit by something which frightens me. You need not worry about my health. My brothers will help me and I will always ask Jesus to give me the strength to pray for you and for all humanity.

A big kiss from me and please pray for me.

Your son,

Padre Pio

The humble friary had already become a 'domain' to Padre Pio. It was to be precisely in this 'domain' that the wonderful thing was to happen which would mark him for life and make him live in the odour of sanctity. It was here, at San Giovanni Rotondo that Padre Pio was to receive the stigmata.

The 'domain' of San Giovanni Rotondo was far removed from the world, accessible only on foot by a stony, dusty little road. Here Padre Pio felt his soul reaching out as he dedicated himself to prayer and meditation, living in communion with nature and with God.

He was on a sunny mountainside, in somewhat wild and arid country, a place of profound silence. In such a place the sounds of the outside world become muffled; there is no danger of their disrupting the atmosphere of peace and serenity.

Then reddish marks on his hands, feet and side became increasingly evident and Padre Pio tried to hide them as best he could from both the guests and from the brothers with whom he joined in prayer several times a day. Meanwhile he ate less and less every day: eating began to be unimportant to the friar from Pietrelcina who looked on it merely as a disagreeable duty, necessary to sustain life. From then on he was to become increasingly immersed in the spiritual life.

25

In the eyes of the world, he became more and more associated with the stigmata. Years later, these red signs of his martyrdom were probably the deciding factor in the opening of the cause for his beatification. For fifty years, they bore unmistakable witness to the physical and spiritual suffering of the friar of Gargano. We shall never know exactly what happened in his body and soul on that 20 September of 1918; it will remain one of the spiritual mysteries of the stigmatists, spiritual giants who are fortunate enough to be in contact with the Lord, witnessing to Christ and proclaiming his saving death as they bear, in this life, the marks of his passion.

Let us see what Padre Pio himself had to say about this miraculous event in three letters; together they make up a remarkable and profoundly human document of the story of his spirituality. It is like looking at a film of the martyrdom of the friar of San Giovanni Rotondo, a martyrdom first of all willed by God and then compounded by human beings who wanted to know all about it and to probe even into that part of the soul which is, or should be, shrouded in mystery. Padre Pio accepted all his sufferings, from God and from human beings, peacefully and joyfully.

By the way of introduction, I quote from a conference on Padre Pio which I was fortunate enough to attend. The speaker was Cardinal Giacomo Lercaro, Archbishop of Bologna:

> It is with a deep sense of humility that I speak to you, brothers of the Capuchin order, faithful members of the prayer groups and all my other brothers and sisters here today. I am humbled by the figure of Padre Pio whose sudden yet expected death, by taking him beyond this world, has at last enabled us all, even his most obstinate adversaries, to perceive his spiritual stature.
>
> I am not going to speak of the strange phenomena which drew the attention of the world to the humble Capuchin of the Gargano friary: the stigmata, the mysterious perfumes, the gifts of prophecy, the ability to read souls. I neither deny nor affirm the reality of all these, I submit them to the discernment and the judgement of the Church and I believe with St Paul that it is not these gifts of the spirit which make him great, because, like all charisms, they are free gifts which the one Lord

26

distributes as he wills; they are given for the good of the spiritual body, that is, the ecclesial community, of which Christ is the head.

Cardinal Lercaro's words are all the more significant when one considers that formerly in that quarter the friar of Gargano was viewed with a certain disapproval.

So even a prince of the Church, a man from the Vatican, could speak of Padre Pio's stigmata with a sense of hidden wonder. Now let us see how Padre Pio himself describes this miraculous event in a letter to Father Benedetto. It was written while Padre Pio was at Pietrelcina on account of his poor health.

Pietrelcina, 8 September 1911

My dear Father,

Please don't be angry if I am a bit late in answering your letter. I was neither reluctant nor unwilling to do so; it is just that I am in the country to get some fresh air, which is already making me better. So it was not until today, when I went to celebrate Mass in the village, that your letter was given to me and I decided to lose no time in answering it.

Yesterday evening something happened to me that I can neither explain nor understand.

Red marks appeared in the middle of the palms of my hands; they are about the size of a cent and in the centre of the red part I feel a very acute pain. This pain was worse in the middle of my left hand and is still there. I also have a bit of pain under my feet.

This has been going on for nearly a year now, but I had not had it for some time until yesterday. Don't be worried by the fact that I'm telling you about it now for the first time; I was always stopped by the wretched shyness of mine. Even now, if you only knew how much it cost me to tell you!

I have a lot to tell you but I don't seem able to put it into words, so I'll just say that my heart beats much faster when I'm in the presence of Jesus in the Blessed Sacrament. Sometimes I think my heart wants to leap out of my breast! At the altar sometimes I feel as if my whole being is on fire – it's indescribable – my face particularly seems to be ablaze.

I don't know what these signs mean, Father. You can imagine how much I want to come back to the friary. Really the greatest sacrifice I've made to the Lord is not having been able to live at the friary. But I don't in the least believe that he actually wants

27

me to die. It's true that I have been ill and am still ill at home but I've never been unable to fulfil my religious duties, which is something I could not manage at the friary. If it were a matter of suffering alone, that would be fine. But to be a burden and nuisance to others and then just to die, seems incomprehensible to me. Besides, I feel I have the right and the duty not to deprive myself of life at the age of 24. It seems that this is what the Lord wants too. But at the moment I seem more dead than alive and, believe me, I am prepared for any sacrifice if it's a question of obedience.

Thank you for the habit. I'll say the five Masses for August and the five for September during this month and at the beginning of next month.

Hoping to hear from you soon, I ask your blessing.

Yours,

Fra Pio

Chapter 8

The stigmata

They appeared and disappeared again: blood stains, acute pains, such were the signs which aroused so much interest in the following years, winning approval or disapproval from doctors, spiritual directors and church authorities. Nearly every week these phenomena appeared and then disappeared again until, in 1918, Padre Pio, who was by then established at San Giovanni Rotondo, received the stigmata that would remain visible until his death. He wrote again of this subject to Father Benedetto on 22 October:

My dear Father,

May Jesus the Sun of righteousness ever shine upon your soul, immersed as it is in the mysterious darkness of the trial he himself directly wills for you. Father, why are you so troubled and fearful in spirit? Be at peace for Jesus is with you and is pleased with you. It breaks my heart to know how much you are suffering spiritually. How I have prayed to Our Lord for you; he tells me in my heart that he is always with you and has poured his grace upon you and loves you with a special love . . .

What can I tell you about what you ask me, how my crucifixion came about?

My God, how confused and humiliated I feel at having to tell others what you have done in this wretched creature of yours!

It was the morning of the 20th of last month. I was in choir after the celebration of holy Mass when I went into a state of quiet similar to a light sleep. All my outer and inner senses were in an indescribable state of repose. In all this there was complete silence all round me. Suddenly this great peace gave way to complete abandonment and I felt as if I were going to cease to exist.

All this took place in a moment. And while all this was happening, I saw in front of me a mysterious Person, like the one I saw on 5 August; the only difference was that this Person had blood dripping from his hands, feet and side.

29

I was terrified when I saw him . . . I couldn't say what I felt at that moment . . . I felt I was dying and I would have died, my heart was beating so violently, had the Lord not come to my aid.

The vision of the Person faded and I saw that my hands, feet and side had been pierced and were dripping blood.

Imagine the agony I felt at that moment and continue to feel, nearly every day; the wound in my breast bleeds copiously, especially from Thursday evening until Saturday.

Father, I am in dreadful pain on account of the torment and subsequent confusion I feel in the depths of my soul! I'm afraid I'll die through loss of blood if the Lord does not hear the cries of my poor heart and stop doing this to me . . .

Will Jesus, who is so good, grant me this grace? Will he at least take away the confusion I feel on account of these signs?

Father, now that you know what is going on inside me, please send me a word of comfort in the midst of such fierce and violent suffering.

I always pray for you, for Father Agostino, for everyone. Please bless your most affectionate son.

Fra Pio

On the evening of 5 August, to which the letter refers, Padre Pio had received the wound in the side which was also bleeding; a mystical phenomenon similar to that experienced by St Teresa of Avila.

Here is the letter he wrote about it to his confessor, Father Agostino:

I was hearing the confessions of our boys on the evening of the 5th when suddenly I was filled with absolute terror at the sight of the heavenly Person who appeared in my mind's eye. He held a sort of weapon in his hands, like a very long iron lance with a well-sharpened point and it seemed as if fire were coming out of the tip. It happened all at the same instant: I saw this Person and he plunged the lance violently into my soul! I hardly moaned, I thought I was dying! I told the boy to go away because I felt ill and did not feel strong enough to go on. This martyrdom continued without a break until the morning of the 7th. I can't tell you what I suffered in that terrible time! My very entrails were wrenched and torn by that weapon and everything in me was put to the sword and plunged into the flames!

From that day to this, I have been mortally wounded. I feel

30

there is a wound in the depths of my soul; it is always open and makes me suffer agonies.

Is this not a new punishment inflicted on me by divine justice? You be the judge of how much truth there is in this and if I have not every reason to fear, when I am in such torment.

I kiss your hand with deep respect, asking your holy blessing.

I remain your son,

Fra Pio

Chapter 9

The mysterious perfume

There has been much discussion of Padre Pio's 'perfume'; some have compared it to violets, others to a mixture of roses and cyclamens and always, for those fortunate enough to sense it, it contained a mysterious message: an invitation, a memory, a call. The faithful who were closest to the friar enjoyed this mystical gift the most often.

Once I was in the old friary church hearing Mass, Padre Pio's long Mass, and just at the elevation of the host, my mind was wandering and I remained standing among the rest of the faithful who were kneeling. Suddenly I was struck by a strong scent of violets which brought me back to reality; looking round me and seeing the crowd kneeling down, I too knelt down, feeling a bit embarrassed but not thinking about the strange perfume. It was after the bell that marked the end of the most important part of the rite, that I looked up at Padre Pio at the altar and began to wonder about the strange perfume. As usual when the service was over I went to greet the friar who asked pointedly,

'So you were a bit distracted today, were you?'

'Yes, Father, I was a bit distracted today. Luckily your perfume woke me up . . .'

'What perfume? What you need is a good smack!'

Padre Pio's perfume, which the faithful of San Giovanni Rotondo call 'the odour of sanctity', has nothing in common with ordinary commercial scents; it is penetrating and unmistakable. Scholars define it as 'osmogenesis.' Several of Padre Pio's confrères, such as Father Agostino da San Marco in Lamis, bore authoritative witness to this phenomenon, as did Doctor Luigi Romanelli (who was asked to confirm the stigmata). In a letter of 7 November 1920 to the father provincial, Pietro da Ischitella, he wrote as follows:

'In June 1919 when I first went to San Giovanni Rotondo,

32

I had hardly been introduced to Padre Pio when I noticed a certain perfume coming from his body; it was so pronounced that I said to the Very Reverend Father E.E. da Valenzano who was with me that it seemed wrong to me that a friar, especially one held in such esteem, should be using perfume. I did not notice any perfume for the next two days of my stay in San Giovanni, even though I was constantly in Padre Pio's company and went into his cell. Before leaving in the afternoon as I went up the stairs I suddenly noticed the same perfume as on the first day but it only lasted a few moments.

Please note, Very Reverend Father, that it was not my imagination; firstly because no one had told me about such a phenomenon and secondly because, had it been mere suggestion on my part, I would have smelt the perfume all the time and not at long intervals. I have wanted to affirm this definitely because it is all too common to say phenomena are a mere suggestion just because they are unexplained and inexplicable.'

Dr Romanelli even told the same Father Provincial that he could 'almost taste' the perfume, it was so strong and penetrating.

Again, Father Raffaele di Sant'Elia who lived with Padre Pio for many years, tells us,

'In choir during the recitation of the divine office we sometimes noticed a very special kind of perfume which came from the wounds on his bleeding hands; I have noticed the same perfume more than once in his cell when I went to talk to him about some sick person. Then one evening after supper while the whole community was on the way to choir for thanksgiving, as is our custom, Padre Pio was ahead of us and as we went downstairs and into the corridor we found that he had left a strong perfume which filled the entire corridor.'

Was this perfume another mystical gift and a sign of Padre Pio's virtue, or rather a special sign for those who had greater faith in him, who followed him and believed in his message of peace and holiness? And if this indefinable essence of cyclamens, roses and violets was perceived also by those without faith, those far from the things of God, what does that mean? It is known that Padre Pio was always very close to the lost sheep, he was gentler and more tolerant

with those of little faith than with others, in order to bring
them back to the Lord. So it was a perfume for all, the good
and the bad, but perhaps it was more penetrating and was
'tasted' more powerfully by those who were far off — and
that authenticates it for me.

Chapter 10

Bilocation

Padre Pio had the gift of bilocation, either physically or by means of the penetrating perfume, sometimes of violets, sometimes of roses or lilies, although it is certain that he never left San Giovanni.

So it came about that one day Padre Pio was looking out of the window; he was completely absorbed and seemed to be miles away and when the younger brothers went by and kissed his hand he murmured the words of absolution. A few days later, a telegram came from Turin thanking him for being with a dying man and helping him to have a holy death.

The marchioness Giovanna Rizzani Boschi was able to tell how Padre Pio had spoken to her of the circumstances of her own birth although he had not been present. 'I entrust this child to you,' Our Lady had said to him in a dream. 'But I can't look after her, I'm too far away!' 'You'll be seeing her here but first you will see her in St Peter's!' answered Our Lady. He also mentioned this episode in one of his writings.

All this is incredible when one thinks that the marchioness Rizzani Boschi did not even know of the existence of Padre Pio until she met him and became his spiritual daughter and co-worker.

This is how the second part of the story took place, the meeting in St Peter's. The marchioness was going round the Basilica of St Peter one evening looking for a priest to discuss some doubts she had about the faith. 'It's late and the church should be closed,' said the sacristan.

Suddenly a young Capuchin friar appeared in a confessional: she spoke to him and was given some reassuring answers. Going back to a friend of hers, she told her about the answers she had received and suggested that she too should go and kiss the friar's hand. But the confessional was empty and the sacristan had not seen any Capuchin friar that day!

Exactly a year later, the marchioness went to San Giovanni Rotondo with an aunt who wanted to make her confession to Padre Pio. When Padre Pio went by in the corridor he suddenly caught sight of her and stared at her. 'I know you! You are Giovanna and you were born the day your father died.' The marchioness was dumbfounded. The next day she went to confess to Padre Pio and asked him how he knew so much about her private life. 'You have already spoken to me, a year ago in St Peter's, remember? I was that Capuchin friar whose advice you asked.'

From that time onwards, the marchioness went more and more often to San Giovanni Rotondo and became one of the most trusted helpers of Padre Pio.

Three days before Padre Pio died, on 19 September, I arrived in San Giovanni with the photographer D'Alessandro. Strangely, the door of the friary church was closed. So we went into the garden where we found a door which opened onto a staircase leading to the friary. We went up and met Padre Pio at the top of the stairs. We knelt down and he laid his hands on our heads in blessing. But Pietro D'Alessandro did not take a single photo, which was very odd because he usually took dozens and normally never missed a chance to have a new record of Padre Pio. D'Alessandro seemed to be troubled about something and he did not use his camera. As we went downstairs looking at each other in surprise, we noticed something else unusual: Padre Pio had not been annoyed at the sight of the camera; he always showed some impatience when he saw a photographer and usually made some angry remark.

As we came out into the square in front of the friary, we met Father Lino da Prato, superior of the Friary of Sant'Anna at Foggia with whom I was on very friendly terms. We told him we had just seen Padre Pio and he said that was impossible: 'Padre Pio is ill, he's been in bed for days.' The photographer and I were dumbfounded: it seemed that at the moment when we had knelt before him, Padre Pio had been elsewhere, in his cell, in full view of witnesses; how was this possible? And yet I remember it quite clearly. There was someone else with me, we were both very young and in the best of health so there was no question of our being mistaken or suffering from delusions or hallucinations. We saw Padre

Pio, we knelt down, we felt his hand on our heads, he blessed us: he was there and somewhere else at the same time.

Those who saw him

Padre Pio was at the deathbed of Monsignor Schinosi, the bishop who had ordained him.

An Italian colonel declared that Padre Pio had been visiting prisoners in India every evening and that he recognized all of them when they came to visit him later.

Don Orione, the founder of the Little Work of Divine Providence, said he had seen Padre Pio in St Peter's at the canonization of St Thérèse of the Child Jesus.

Mother Speranza, foundress of the Handmaidens of Merciful Love, who died in the odour of sanctity, told how she had seen Padre Pio every day for a whole year in Rome. We know very well that Padre Pio did not go to Rome except in 1917 when he took one of his sisters there as she had decided to enter an enclosed monastery.

General Luigi Cadorna became so depressed after the defeat of Caporetto that he wanted to take his own life. One night he retired to his apartment and gave orders to his attendant not to admit any callers. He went into his room and took a revolver out of a drawer. As he was pointing it at his head, an unknown voice spoke, 'Come now, General, you're not going to do anything so foolish, are you?!' The general was astonished to see a friar standing there and changed his mind about committing suicide. But how could this person have got into his room? He questioned his orderly but he said that he had seen no one entering or leaving! Years later, the general read a newspaper about a miracle-working friar living on Gargano. He went to San Giovanni incognito and to his amazement recognized the friar as the Capuchin who had visited him on that evening when he was about to kill himself.

'We had a narrow escape that evening, eh General!' whispered Padre Pio.

Chapter 11

The enemies of Padre Pio

Padre Pio's calvary began when he received the stigmata. His physical sufferings were intense because in addition to the acute pain caused by the wounds, he was weakened by the loss of blood. His suffering was intense, which he makes quite plain in a letter to his parents on 26 September 1918, a few days after this extraordinary experience.

My dearest parents,
I am writing this to you with a broken heart, in the most terrible anguish. What can I say to you when each word sticks in my throat because I am suffering so intensely?
My dear ones, the pain is so terrible and so bitter that I have no strength . . . But you are infinite, O Lord, and your judgements are just. God gave me my sister and he has taken her away again, may I bless his holy name! By repeating these words in a state of resignation, I find the strength I need not to faint under the burden of my suffering. I am very miserable indeed . . . and sad that I am unable to come home for a few days so that we could share our grief and pain together; I feel very ill and unable to make such a long and arduous journey. Please don't worry about me as I am out of danger now.
You need not be alarmed when you hear about my state of health as this was exceptional and I am actually healthier at the moment than the other brothers living with me here. Write soon and give me details about my sister and also about your health and mother's as well.
A big kiss from me, and I pray that God will give you every comfort.
Your son
Padre Pio

But the greatest suffering he had to bear was the mental anguish caused by the reactions of certain people as the news of the stigmata gradually came to public notice. There were many who doubted the authenticity of the phenomena and some who thought it was outright trickery.

Padre Pio was very harsh in his condemnation of those who showed no repentance for their sins and those who failed to fulfil their priestly vocation in a worthy manner; so he had lost no time in making various enemies in San Giovanni Rotondo, especially among the local secular clergy. His aversion to certain priests of whose conduct he disapproved led to a real campaign against him. Among his bitterest enemies the most implacable was Monsignor Pasquale Gagliardi, archbishop of Manfredonia, who declared in the Consistorial Congregation at Rome, 'Padre Pio is possessed by the devil and the friars of San Giovanni Rotondo are a crowd of impostors.'

Obviously at this point the Holy See was obliged to take a closer look at the stigmatic friar. It went about this task with its customary caution but also in that spirit of severity which is essential for any organization dealing with the difficult area of supernatural phenomena, something which can cause deep disturbance among the faithful.

It was precisely the more simple among the faithful, the devout masses, who were ready to accept the authenticity of the stigmata without the least hesitation but his enemies opposed him at every turn. There was no denying the presence of the wounds in the friar's hands, feet and side so they said it was nothing but hysteria or even that they were culpably self-inflicted. Padre Pio's suffering became intense. In addition to his physical agony he had to bear the pain of feeling judged and condemned, despite his innocence. Then science came on the scene and took possession of the 'Padre Pio phenomenon'. Doctors and scientists sent by the Vatican and by religious organizations came to San Giovanni Rotondo to investigate and set up stringent tests designed to explode the myth of the stigmata 'given' to Padre Pio. One of these, Luigi Bignami, professor of pathology at the University of Rome, wrote in 1919: 'On the palm of the right hand there is a round, blackish scar, partly detached from the skin beneath; it is very soft and comprises the dermis and possibly the uppermost part of the epidermis and is very clearly defined. The surrounding skin looks normal and is unaffected except for a narrow band of deep yellow colour all round the scar area. An identical but more superficial scar can be seen on the back of the hand in the area corresponding to that of the palm. The skin is unbroken.'

During this scientific investigation, before leaving Padre Pio, Professor Bignami asked severely, 'Padre, why did these wounds appear just on your hands, feet and side rather than in some other part of your body?' To which Padre Pio answered very gently, 'You're a scientist, can you tell me why these wounds should have appeared in another part of my body?'

This is what Doctor Luigi Romanelli, administrator of Barletta Hospital, had to say about Padre Pio's stigmata, 'When I first examined Padre Pio the wound in his chest presented a clean cut seven or eight centimetres long parallel to the ribs and bleeding profusely. When I first saw the lesions in his hands they were covered with a thin membrane of reddish brown colour. I believe, or rather I am certain, that the wounds were not superficial because when I exerted pressure with my fingers, gripping the whole palm, I had an impression of emptiness between my fingers; in fact I had an exact idea of the space between the two lesions.'

These two essentially contradictory reports failed to satisfy the Holy See, so in 1919 they sent a Roman professor, Giorgio Festa, to San Giovanni Rotondo. He was to examine Padre Pio at frequent intervals between 1919 and 1938, sending periodical scientific reports to the Holy See. In one of these reports we read, 'As I was examining the wounds on the hands and feet, small drops of blood were continually oozing from the edges . . . In order to take a good look at Padre Pio's lesions, I helped him to take off his gloves myself and I immediately saw that they were soaked in bloody serum.' And again, 'In one conversation I had with him on the subject, Padre Pio's superior declared, "If higher authority were to question me on this point, I would have to say that when I looked at the wounds on his palms I could easily discern some kind of impression made at the same place on the opposite side of the hand; I'm so certain of this that I would affirm it under oath." '

But the examinations, investigations and scepticism continued. This was source of continual mortification to Padre Pio; he accepted it out of obedience but it left him deeply depressed in spirit. Witness this letter of 25 August 1920, written once more to his confessor Father Agostino di San Marco in Lamis:

My dear Father,

What shall I say to you about my spiritual state? I am extremely desolate. I feel afflicted and tormented as I seem to be alone in bearing everyone's burdens. I suffer agonies, it wears me out and breaks my heart to think that I am unable to bring spiritual help to those to whom Jesus sends me. So many souls are irresponsible, seeking to justify the wrong they do, disregarding the absolute holiness of God.

Recently I have been overwhelmingly and most painfully conscious of two apparently contradictory forces within me: one is the desire to live in order to help my exiled brothers and sisters and the other is the wish to die in order to be united with my Spouse. All this tears me apart and although it does not destroy my inner peace, it does cause me outward disquiet, robbing me of that outward calm which is so necessary if I am to be more gentle in my dealings with others.

Please Father, don't leave me alone! Help me with your prayers. All this is making me lose my peace and rest and even my appetite . . .

I kiss your hand respectfully and ask your blessing.

Your son
Padre Pio

It was difficult for people to accept the truly supernatural nature of the stigmata. Many continued to doubt, which gave rise to further investigations. The day came, however, when the Vatican decided to stop sending doctors; none of them was permitted to go near Padre Pio any longer; even Father Agostino Gemelli, the founder of the Catholic University of Milan, was firmly refused entrance when he presented himself at the friary. On that occasion, Father Gemelli wrote in the visitors' book, 'Each day the Franciscan tree bears fresh fruit and this is the greatest comfort to those who draw life from this wonderful tree.' These words were not written in defence of Padre Pio, seeing that Father Gemelli was one of those who strongly held the stigmata to be hysterical in origin, although he had never been able to see them. And his opinion certainly influenced subsequent decisions taken by the Vatican.

In 1923, during the pontificate of Pius XI, a decree from

41

the Holy Office declared that after thorough investigation it had been concluded that the phenomena attributed to Padre Pio could not be considered as supernatural and therefore the faithful were asked to act in accordance with this authoritative statement. This document is part of the *Acta Apostolicae Sedis*. When a friar told Padre Pio about the contents, he showed no surprise and exclaimed, 'I am only too happy to suffer from the wounds in my wretched body but how I wish these wounds were not seen by other people; it embarrasses me so much.'

Thus Padre Pio's enemies and persecutors got what they wanted; he was placed under restriction. He was no longer allowed to celebrate Mass publicly, he could no longer hear confessions or give counsel to the faithful, he was even forbidden to write letters. It was as if he were in prison, without even the daily hour of fresh air allowed to prisoners. Even his spiritual exercises came under the ban of the Holy Office, those exercises which were like manna from heaven to him, a sweet penance; but how could anyone restrict such exercises when his whole day was dedicated to the Lord and every moment was a deep and mysterious spiritual exercise?

The faithful, however, showed no signs of lessening their devotion to Padre Pio and in 1942 the Holy Office issued a strict order forbidding them to 'visit Padre Pio "*devotionis causa*" and to have any dealings with him, even by letter.'

There was also an attempt to transfer him elsewhere but the people rose up in weeping protest, begging the friary not to let the friar be sent away. Although he had various enemies, Padre Pio also had many people who were loyal to him, who appreciated his generosity and the importance of his apostolate. Already there were scattered reports of miracles worked through his intercession; from then on, his fame was universal.

In the wake of these events, Monsignor Felice Bevilacqua made an apostolic visit to San Giovanni Rotondo in 1927 and initiated a proper and thorough inquiry into the friary and everything connected with it. One of Padre Pio's spiritual sons, Emanuele Brunatto, helped him in this task. At the end of this delicate mission, the archbishop of Manfredonia, Monsignor Gagliardi, a bitter opponent of Padre

Pio, was removed from office along with several other priests. The followers of Padre Pio breathed a sigh of relief but the restrictions on the stigmatic friar continued.

Another six years went by and only on 16 July 1933, after several observers sent by Pius XI had expressed themselves in his favour, did the Pope issue a decree from the Holy Office permitting Padre Pio to resume public celebration of the Mass. Then, a year later, came the permission for him to hear confessions again. And immediately there were huge crowds outside his confessional.

It was during this difficult period of the friar's life that his mother died, on 29 January 1929. He was in his cell, deep in prayer, when they told him the sad news. Padre Pio burst into floods of tears, crying out his mother's name in a frenzy of grief. When his brothers gathered round him and tried to calm him by reminding him how he himself had condemned similar outbursts of grief, he answered through his sobs, 'You're right but now I understand the pain of losing a loved one, the person one loved most!'

Chapter 12

The real miracle: the House for the Relief of Suffering*

'No, I don't want coffins coming out of my House for the Relief of Suffering', exclaimed Padre Pio one May morning in 1966. He was standing looking at the great hospital from a cell in the friary as a hearse prepared to take up the coffin. So saying, he put his head in his hands and remained like that for a few moments, leaning against the pane of the small window until Father Onorato led him away, saying, 'But, Father, sick people die too'. Padre Pio looked at him hard and answered almost in a tone of rebuke, 'What are you saying, what do you know about sick people? We need many doctors, and good ones, too . . .!'

In years to come, the story of the House of Relief of Suffering will become a legend just because it is a story full of symbolism. This hospital complex, unique in all Europe, rose out of the bare rock in a poor district and was inspired by a penniless friar.

It was a very cold evening in January 1940. Padre Pio's visitors were telling him the latest news of the war; he was thinking of the soldiers suffering both physically and spiritually on the various fronts: brothers fighting against brothers. Italy had not yet been swept into the vortex of the Second World War but there were already alarming signs that the country would soon be involved.

Turning to the local doctor, Gugliemo Sanguinetti, who on that evening of 9 January was in the friar's small cell with Mario Sanvico and Carlo Kiswaroaj, Padre Pio exclaimed,

---

*Padre Pio, the great apostle of suffering, used to repeat, 'Those who overcome themselves and bend over their unfortunate brothers and sisters, lift up to the Lord the most noble of prayers, made up of sacrifice and living love.' And again, 'In every sick person, Jesus suffers! In every poor person, Jesus is in need! In every sick person who is also poor, Jesus is doubly present, in pain and in poverty!'

'This evening my poor earthly task is beginning.' And immediately afterwards he added, 'What a horrible thing war is! I pity the poor mothers' sons who die but even worse are those who are permanently affected physically! In every person who suffers physically, Jesus suffers.'

And again, as he fingered his rosary and looked out of the tiny window of his cell, the stigmatic friar gave a start, 'Oh those poor people who suffer bodily pain, those disinherited ones who don't know how to alleviate their anguish! How many there will be here, how many all over the world who lie there, deprived of all comfort. Jesus loved the poor; Jesus is in all poor people who suffer; in all those who are both poor and sick Jesus suffers twice over.' And looking straight at the doctor before him, he said, 'Let's hope that the good Jesus will help us to relieve the sufferings of the sick poor!'

So it was in a cold and narrow cell that the idea of the House for the Relief of Suffering was born. It was to be Padre Pio's pride and joy but also a great source of suffering and adversity in his earthly life.

The first donation was made by the friar himself in the shape of a small gold coin he received as an alms from a poor old woman in early 1940. 'This is the first stone of a great hospital we are going to build here,' said Padre Pio, turning to Doctor Sanguinetti again and pointing to the small coin which shone in his bandaged hand. When Doctor Sanvico asked him a few days later what he was going to call the project, he answered: The House for the Relief of Suffering.

As Padre Pio saw it, human beings suffered both in body and spirit but whilst great faith was necessary to alleviate spiritual distress, when it came to physical suffering, as well as faith and hope one also needed human endeavour.

It was with these considerations in mind that Padre Pio started his grandiose project. He wanted to alleviate the physical aliments of the poor without their having to worry about money. He could have called it a 'hospital for the poor' but for Padre Pio there were no class distinctions: all were equal in the sight of God, all were equal in the face of physical suffering! Yet in all written histories of the House for the Relief of Suffering there is no mention of the stigmatic friar's dearest wish which was to treat the poor free of charge.

Naturally enough, Padre Pio's idea soon attracted other people. Among the hospital's first benefactors were Elena Bandini, Dr Sanvico, Ida Seitz, Davide Ancona, Ettore Masone, Silvio Zeni, Antonio Massa, Cleonice Morcaldi, Doctor Kappaiswarday and a blind man, Pietro Cuggino. The total sum collected was 967 lire. It was the first step in a project that was to cost millions. Padre Pio was full of hope: human charity could work the miracle. Sure enough, the first fairly substantial contributions towards the building of the House for the Relief of Suffering began to arrive at San Giovanni Rotondo. The mayor of New York, Fiorello La Guardia, who came from Foggia, sent 250,000,000 lire, thus starting a series of donations which continued to come from the United States and from every corner of the globe.

From then on, Padre Pio's truly miraculous project gave rise to great enthusiasm, but also to a certain puzzlement, all over the world. The money was there; all that was needed was someone who could actually build the hospital. Padre Pio did not contact engineers or architects nor did he announce a competition for the design of the building. One day he called a certain Angelo Lupi, a native of Pescara, into his cell and asked him to become involved in the construction of the House for the Relief of Suffering. Lupi was not an engineer; he simply had a very strong will and great creative ability, but besides these gifts he was deeply devoted to Padre Pio and he had a profound faith in divine providence. And divine providence was not slow to intervene: on 5 May 1956 the enormous hospital complex was inaugurated by Cardinal Giacomo Lercaro who said, 'The finger of God is here! Have you become aware of this at San Giovanni Rotondo? The whole world has become aware of it.'

And during an audience granted to the directors of the House, Pius XII declared, 'The hospital of San Giovanni Rotondo which is now opening its doors for the first time, is the fruit of deep intuition, the outcome of an ideal matured and perfected by constant contact with the most varied and cruel aspects of human suffering, both moral and physical. Those who are called in a professional capacity to heal souls and bodies, soon realize to what extent bodily pain, in all

46

its forms, pervades the whole personality, deeply affecting moral attitudes; this obliges us to confront afresh the fundamental problems of life: attitudes to God and human beings, collective and individual responsibility, the sense of being pilgrims here on earth.'

Padre Pio's grandiose idea was now a reality. The House for the Relief of Suffering was born and at once the leading figures in world medicine decided to help in the work, either on a temporary basis or permanently. Today, thirty years after its inauguration, the House for the Relief of Suffering has the most sophisticated technical and scientific equipment and the most up-to-date hygienic and sanitary systems; it is still expanding as the beds available fail to keep pace with the constant demand for healing.

Chapter 13

The new enemies of Padre Pio

I said that the only time I left San Giovanni Rotondo sad at heart was when Padre Pio could do nothing for the seriously ill child of a colleague of mine.

That is true, but Padre Pio was hard on me on many other occasions; some times he even threw me out but I never felt bitter or miserable, partly because I knew he would receive me differently the next time I went and partly because at bottom I felt a bit guilty. That was because when he threw me out it was always because I had annoyed him by going to see him with a photographer. He did not like the flash and all the photographic equipment; it upset him, above all because he wanted to avoid anything that would increase the fame and publicity attached to his name. For my part, I had seen from the start how the magnificent medium of the press could carry Padre Pio's message far beyond San Giovanni Rotondo, beyond the bounds of Puglia. And, above all, accurate information about him would give the lie to all the untrue stories which were continually turning up in various branches of the mass media. However, it was difficult to carry out these intentions of mine in view of the friar's unfavourable attitude to the press and I was unable to make new excuses every time; when I told him a lie, I could not stand up to his penetrating gaze. Despite all this and thanks to the help of my friends among the friars, I did succeed in writing a number of articles on Padre Pio. In 1960 for example, when there was talk of transferring him as far away as Spain, it was I who gave notice of this in a Roman daily paper, *Telesera*. (And perhaps the fact that I had leaked the news ahead of time was a help towards having the decision reversed.)

That was a time of constant calumny and accusations levelled against a man who had dedicated his whole life to the welfare of others, a man who inspired such confidence that he received donations for his work from all over the world. He received so many donations because his project was great and generous and had aroused enormous enthusiasm in people of every continent and social background. But the very fact that he did receive so much money was a source of fresh humiliation and suffering for Padre Pio.

In fact certain unscrupulous people eagerly seized on these donations. Sad to say, some of his fellow friars were among them. These religious were more naive than wicked; finding themselves in financial difficulties, at a certain point they realized that in order to recuperate certain grievous and unforeseen losses, they would have to dip into Padre Pio's donations. It was the only way to balance their books. And the poor innocent friar found himself involved in the furore.

Let us hear what Cardinal Lercaro had to say on this subject: 'Was it surprising that Padre Pio was saddened, deeply pained, to find that people who had no right to do so, were trying to appropriate the funds of the House for the Relief of Suffering, funds which had been donated through the charity of his spiritual sons and daughters? . . . Certainly he was right in his humble but firm defence of the interests of those who had made donations. He was right to safeguard the money entrusted to him; despite his vow of poverty, he had a duty to dispose of his own property unless or until obedience to higher authority relieved him of his responsibility for the project.

But the thing that wounded him to the quick and made him agonize like the Saviour in the Garden of Olives, was the fact that he was not suffering for the Church — that would have been a comfort to him, as the Bible promises a blessing to those who suffer for the sake of the Gospel — no, he was suffering from the Church. Now the Church is a community transformed by the Spirit of Christ into a wonderful sacrament of salvation and it was the churchmen themselves who were polluting this community with their wretched greed, ambition, meaness and dishonesty . . . He knew the bitterness of arbitrary procedures, harsh dealings, insults and scorn but he endured his cruel sufferings without complaint or retaliation . . . he was isolated from his friends and like Jesus he could say, "I looked in vain for someone to comfort me" . . . Instead of friends he had enemies, wretched, mediocre types who could not bear the sight of a more virtuous man. His own brothers who had hitherto been his strength and stay, actually became his tormentors and those who, according to Capuchin tradition, should have been a support to him in his old age, miserably betrayed him with the sacrilegious kiss of the traitor . . .'

Certainly Padre Pio was not one who was attached to worldly goods. Following the most rigorous rules of asceticism, it might be said that he lived on 'nothing'. The problem of donations was one which had arisen very early in his ministry. He started receiving money from 1919 onwards and at that time the idea of the House for the Relief of Suffering was well in the future. The first thing he had done was to ask advice of his spiritual father as to how he should use this money, as we can see in this letter of 16 November 1919:

My dear Father,

May Jesus grant you more abundant blessings and make you ever more dear to him.

I should have written to you earlier to thank you for all you have done for me, especially during your last stay with us and for the great concern you showed about my recent illness. May Jesus reward you richly; I pray for you continually.

I regard your advice and suggestions as well as the fatherly rebukes which you made to me in person as absolutely binding on me and with God's help I will do my best to act in accordance with them. I regret that I involuntarily and inadvertently raised my voice several times while I was being corrected. I know this is a reprehensible weakness but how can I avoid it if it happens without my being aware of it? Still, I pray and complain to the Lord about this but he has not yet answered my prayer completely. And in spite of all the care I take over this, sometimes I find myself doing what I hate and wish to avoid. Please commend me continually to the divine mercy.

Now I would like to ask you to clear up a few points. If a secular person gives us religious any sum of money, requesting us to use it as we judge best, for the glory of God and the relief of our neighbour, is it against our rule if the religious to whom such a sum is given, under such conditions, uses the offering as he thinks fit in good conscience? Is it in order for us to mention the names of poor people to the rich so that they may be helped in their need? If someone comes and gives us an offering earmarked for the relief of the poor, is it right for us to use it in that way? Please would you advise me on these points? I kiss your hand and ask your holy blessing.

Padre Pio

Thirty years after this ingenuous request for direction on the part of the friar, the banker Giovanni Battista Giuffré from Bologna appeared on the scene. He had developed a banking method called 'lend and increase' with very high interest rates, from forty to a hundred per cent, with the apparent intention of financing charitable works in northern Italy.

Soon he was so deeply in debt that 'God's banker' (as he was dubbed by the press when the scandal broke) did not know where to turn but a certain individual who had profited by his generosity thought he could very likely get hold of some of the money Padre Pio had received for the House for the Relief of Suffering. These were unscrupulous people, of course, people who, it must be said, hoped to profit from the various schemes put forward by Giuffré's opponents. Pope Pius XII himself, when notified of the banker's plight, issued a serious warning to the bishops to 'avoid all dealings with Giuffré'.

Padre Pio also, when he found out about the banker's activities, put his own brothers on guard against 'engaging in speculation lest you end up breaking not only civil law but also transgressing against Canon Law and Holy Scripture.'

But all the warnings were in vain. Speculation continued and the banking corporation ended in complete financial disaster. Things moved quickly, leading to ruin and disaster in the areas where Giuffré had been operative. Individuals, corporations and religious communities were upset when the Bolognese banker crashed.

But, as a dear friend of Padre Pio wrote, 'Padre Pio is always ready to use any of his reserve funds to help those in financial distress or to come to the aid of those overtaken by sudden misfortune; he takes to heart the troubles of the many people who have been ruined by the collapse of that banking corporation and is himself disturbed and upset by it.' But the news concerning the Franciscan order saddened him most of all. At one point the word went out that the

51

monastic province of Foggia was in considerable difficulty as a result of the collapse of the banking corporation.

Unfortunately it was not just a rumour. The religious of the province of Foggia, who had already received considerable loans from Padre Pio, asked for more in order to repair the damage caused by their participation in the Giuffré affair, which had ended in such disaster. They even had recourse to threats and applied various pressures in order to obtain funds. In the end they succeeded in obtaining a loan of forty million lire from the House for the Relief of Suffering — with Padre Pio's knowledge — which they undertook to repay in a short time. Padre Pio felt that his confrères had made a mistake and he wished to help them out of it (perhaps even more, he wished to safeguard the good name of the order to which he belonged); that was the only fault of the 'saint of San Giovanni' and he was criticized and persecuted as a result. There was talk of irregularity in the management of the House for the Relief of Suffering, of 'speculators living under the protection of Padre Pio'.

A second period of intense suffering began for Padre Pio with the apostolic visit of Monsignor Maccari who was sent to San Giovanni Rotondo by the Vatican. The press got hold of the news and unleashed a series of speculations and rumours, insinuations and half-truths. It was the time when all the friar's incoming mail was intercepted. All the letters sent from all over the world to the 'saint of Gargano' were seized, without regard either for him or for the faithful who wrote to him, which prevented the friar from responding personally to the many requests he received.

After stopping at Foggia to speak to the father provincial and at Manfredonia to see the archbishop, the Vatican envoy arrived at San Giovanni Rotondo to find Padre Pio at a very low ebb. Perhaps it was the first time he had felt completely abandoned and maybe on this occasion he prayed for 'our sister the death of the body'.

Monsignor Maccari installed himself in the House for the Relief of Suffering in order to gain first-hand knowledge of this magnificent hospital and at the same time to look into long-standing allegations concerning the misappropriation of funds received by San Giovanni Rotondo. So a fresh inquiry, or rather 'inquisition', began and the accusations so long levelled against the stigmatic friar were once more subjected to the glare of publicity.

The Vatican envoy approached all the local clergy and questioned them at length, seeking to understand and weigh the import of all they said – or did not say – on the subject. When he spoke to one of the brothers at the Friary of Our Lady of Grace and asked a rather insulting question about Padre Pio's life, the friar became violently angry, firmly and scornfully rejecting all criticisms of the integrity and uprightness of the humble friar. And when the 'inquisitor' tried to find out about the present affairs of San Giovanni Rotondo, the friar smiled and exclaimed, 'But even the Pope knows what's going on here!' As for the religious fanaticism prevalent in the Gargano area, he said it was scarcely to be wondered at because wherever anything disturbing or mysterious happens, there is bound to be a certain reaction on the part of the masses.

One priest was transferred to another parish because he was too enthusiastic about Padre Pio, while on the other hand another priest, without proper authority, chose to play private detective: he was the secretary of the apostolic nuncio and began to visit bars, private houses and businesses asking questions and finding out what local people felt about the 'Padre Pio phenomenon'. But nothing concrete emerged from this visit to San Giovanni Rotondo, not even when they opened all the letters which arrived in their hundreds at the local post office. In the end, seeing no chance of proving any charge against Padre Pio, Monsignor Maccari decided to speak to him personally.

When they met the atmosphere was rather frosty but it was the friar himself who broke the ice by exclaiming, 'Blessed are the prisoners because at least they know how long they have to spend in prison. They have a fixed sentence, but as for me . . .!' No one ever knew what was said in that long conversation on a hot August day in 1960, but shortly afterwards, before returning to Rome, Monsignor Maccari told the brothers at the friary that Padre Pio would not be transferred to Spain, contrary to what he called 'journalistic suggestions'.

I remember how pleased I was to hear this news. Naturally

I was at San Giovanni, anxiously awaiting the outcome of the enquiry held by the apostolic visitor. Having myself announced the possibility of a transfer, I was in fact keen to keep track of developments for my paper and I felt it incumbent upon me to keep my readers informed since I had told them of the danger in which Padre Pio stood. This is what I wrote on that occasion: 'Padre Pio will not be transferred either to Spain or to the Vatican: Monsignor Maccari made a statement to this effect to a group of the faithful who were anxiously asking about this rumour reported in the press. The secretary general of the Holy See assured the faithful of San Giovanni Rotondo that Padre Pio will be carrying on his religious duties without hindrance; he added that Padre Pio's presence at San Giovanni was justified as it was normal for a friar to spend some time in a centre of pilgrimage, quite apart from the call of his administrative duties at the House for the Relief of Suffering which, as is well known, lies in the administrative and financial jurisdiction of the Vatican.

As readers will remember, news of the new atmosphere abroad in the small Gargano village was reported some time ago in this newspaper. 'They want to take Padre Pio away' was the headline of the article and the first alarm signal came in the form of an iron railing which was set up, one fine morning between the old and the new parts of the Church of Our Lady of Grace. There was talk of transfer, or rather expulsion, of father guardians and father superiors, whereas up to now only one father guardian and two Capuchins have been transferred for no specific reason. The people of San Giovanni Rotondo became even more alarmed when they were granted only limited access to the Church of Our Lady of Grace. In fact the church door remains closed for several hours a day. All these precautionary measures led to wild speculation in many minds.

If it is true that certain speculations arose, we should try to see how and under what circumstances this happened. Let us start by saying that a great deal of money is sent to San Giovanni Rotondo for charitable purposes. Last year in Foggia there was a court case brought against seven post office employees who had stolen money sent in envelopes addressed to Padre Pio. Scandal was already in the air;

inspectors came from the ministry and, after thorough investigations, brought the dishonest men to justice. Now let us ask ourselves: what does Padre Pio have to do with these suspicious activities which are disturbing the peace around San Giovanni Rotondo?

If there is any speculation in the small Gargano village, it is being started by unscrupulous folk who are using Padre Pio's name to serve their own ends. That is the case with some ten people who send picture postcards of the stigmatic friar all over the world, saying that they will be happy to receive guests desiring private conversation or even confession with Padre Pio. A great many people are taken in by this and sometimes send large sums of money for the services advertised.

Meanwhile, Signor Battisti, administrator of the House for the Relief of Suffering at San Giovanni Rotondo, in a statement issued to the press, mentioned certain circumstances which led to the 'apostolic visitation'; in particular he said, 'I can confirm that all donations received from whatever source have always been officially registered and scrupulously administered; fees and salaries have been paid regularly; I and my closest collaborators, in accordance with the mandate entrusted to us by Padre Pio, have never received the slightest personal profit of any kind.'

The friar of Gargano never saw the huge sums entrusted to him for his work even though he was dispensed, by papal decree, from the vow of poverty: when they arrived, the donations were entrusted to the administrators of the House.

Monsignor Maccari, then, found no trace of illicit dealings on the part of the 'saint of San Giovanni' — how could it be otherwise? — but that did not mean that all suspicion was allayed. The father superior was instructed to impose certain restrictions on the stigmatic friar and thus, at the time of Pope John XXIII's revolutionary Second Vatican Council, Padre Pio was notified of the serious measures formally taken by the Holy Office on 21 January 1961. The times and order of confessions were changed. The Mass, also, had to be celebrated at different times. Padre Pio suffered in silence and continued his works of apostolate among the thousands of faithful who flocked to him.

Emanuele Brunatto, the same spiritual son who had

defended Padre Pio against the Archbishop of Manfredonia's accusations in 1927, collaborated with some of the friar's most faithful followers in preparing a white paper in his defence. This caused quite an uproar because it contained an account of several hitherto unknown episodes of Padre Pio's life, along with certain clear photographic evidence of persecution of the friar who stood out in all his humility and innocence. Meanwhile Padre Pio, who had not written letters for many years, under the pressure of great distress wrote the following to his former superior, Father Carmelo da Sessano del Molise:

Dear Father,
    May the Lord be with you and bless you in your work. Please excuse my bad writing, but my hand will not do what I tell it. What shall I say to you about my life at the moment? I always beg Our Lady to give me strength to bear all that happens to me with fortitude. Sometimes, however, I feel depressed and I put this down to my state of health, which is not very good. I'm never free of my cough, and asthma makes it hard for me to breathe. You have not been here for a long time. How are things going in your 'oasis'? I will also pray that your work will be crowned with success so that you will be able to help many souls in your area. Please pray for my invalids and for me, too.
                            With my blessing,
                            Padre Pio

The 'oasis' Padre Pio was referring to was a large construction bravely undertaken by Father Carmelo da Sessano; this priest had spent years building a home, brick by brick, for poor orphan boys who were educated and then taught a trade in a poor and depressed district in Molise in the south of Italy. Padre Pio showed a keen interest in this project and later a monument to him was built in the square facing the home.

On 17 November 1961, the ownership of the assets of the House for the Relief of Suffering was transferred directly to the Church. But that certainly presented no problem to Padre Pio. In fact he himself had given the deeds of this House to the pope in 1957. What mattered most to him was that the hospital should function ever more efficiently with the help of the donations received. He did not and could never have had any other interest in it.

Chapter 14

Padre Pio's donations

It is somewhat superfluous to point out that Padre Pio had no personal interest in the money he received daily. His one interest, to which he dedicated his whole life, was doing good. That was the reason he had for the House for the Relief of Suffering and that was why he was concerned that his project should continue to run smoothly even after his death.

In 1954 Pius XII had dispensed him from the vow of poverty simply to enable him to administer the monetary affairs of the House. But Padre Pio was so concerned with the success of his project that in 1957 he wrote the following letter to the Pope in which he expressed his intention of handing over the ownership of the House to the Holy See.

'When addressing some of the world's most famous doctors who took part in the symposium on coronary diseases at San Giovanni Rotondo, Your Holiness defined the purpose of the House for the Relief of Suffering in the following words: "it seeks to introduce a more profoundly human and also more supernatural approach to the care of the sick; to provide ideal conditions both from the material and moral points of view, which will enable patients to see the healing team as God's helpers, intent on opening souls to the workings of grace."

The House is run according to two principles: (a) free care for the poor and moderate fees for those who can afford it; (b) no class distinction among patients.

Up until now, the House for the Relief of Suffering has been operated as a shareholders' company according to Italian law; this was the form the project originally took and it was intended as a temporary state of affairs, while the building was under construction.

Holy Father, to enable the House for the Relief of

Suffering to fulfil the Christian purposes for which it was founded, I humbly beg You to grant Your sovereign sanction to the following proposals:

a) to entrust the administration of the House for the Relief of Suffering to the Congregation of the Franciscan Third Order of Our Lady of Grace at San Giovanni Rotondo (Foggia) who will run the hospital according to the norms set out in b) and c). (This Congregation was set up by the Father General with the consent of His Lordship the Bishop of Manfredonia and was recognized as being under his personal jurisdiction by the President of the Italian Republic by the decree of 20 June 1955);

b) In order to administer the House according to the good pleasure of the tertiaries and in keeping with the mandate entrusted to him by them, the undersigned wishes to act as Director of the Congregation (a task already imposed on him by the Father General's decree of 25 August 1954) and, by Your Apostolic indult, to remain in the office of Director during his natural life;

c) to carry out the above-mentioned administration with the good offices of members of the aforesaid Third Order working in consultative committees (medical, cultural, administrative) under the statutory regulations binding on the Third Order for its other activities undertaken outside the House for the Relief of Suffering in accordance with the norms set down in article 2 of the Statutes;

d) to regularize the status of the property by registering with the Institute of Religious Works according to the conditions outlined in the attached paper.

Lastly, I beg You, most Holy Father, to accept the assets of the House for the Relief of Suffering as a gift to the Holy See at my death, if possible using these assets to continue this work.'

The following is the text of the document attached to the letter in which Padre Pio reveals his intention of entrusting the ownership of the House to the Institute of Religious Works while himself retaining the administration:

'Padre Pio da Pietrelcina asks permission to place the stocks representing the total fixed assets of the Society of the

House for the Relief of Suffering in the care of the Institute of Religious Works.

At the time of deposit the assets of the aforesaid Society will be composed solely of fixed assets (without liability) effectively used for religious and charitable works.

The balance-sheet of the Society will take the extremely simple form of a construction company. Such a balance-sheet, drawn up by the competent fiscal authorities, will, as before, be subject to eventual inspection.

The administration of assets is entrusted in due legal form to another corporation canonically instituted for the purpose.

Padre Pio da Pietrelcina asks that the assets at his disposal be placed to the credit of an account in the name of Padre Pio da Pietrelcina for the House for the Relief of Suffering.

Padre Pio will have full rights of disposal of the said deposits and in due time the Holy See will inherit such rights.

The undersigned hereby declares that he intends to leave (according to his lawfully made last will and testament) to the Holy See the assets of which he asks to dispose and whatever further assets there may be in deposit at the time of his death or after his death, in the account in question.'

This was the Vatican's reply:

Very Reverend Father,

The Supreme Pontiff has received with special solicitude the devout and zealous request Your Reverence saw fit to make to Him recently.

In order to give the House for the Relief of Suffering a legal status in keeping both with its purpose and the patronage of the Holy See, His Holiness has most graciously requested the following conditions:

1) that the administration of the House for the Relief of Suffering be entrusted to the Congregation of the Franciscan Third Order of Our Lady of Grace, duly instituted to this end.

2) that Your Reverence should maintain during your natural life the office − presently held by you − of Director of the aforesaid Congregation, administering the House for the Relief of Suffering with the expert co-operation of members of the Third Order;

3) that the stocks representing the fixed assets of the Society of the House for the Relief of Suffering should be deposited with the Institute of Religious Works.

I am happy to inform you that His Holiness, considering the importance of the hospital complex and the excellence of its aims, is graciously pleased to grant you the favours you requested.

However it is to be understood that, in accordance with Italian civil law, the stocks deposited with the Institute for Religious Works should be for the most part accredited to the aforesaid Institute, a lesser portion being placed with another legal office to be named by the same Institute.

On the other hand, as regards the monies destined for the maintenance of the hospital property, His Holiness will have the right to deposit the same with the Institute of Religious Works, restricting their use to the purpose above-mentioned.

It is not, however, deemed advisable to transfer the ownership of stocks or movable of assets to the Holy See. Your Reverence might see fit to accord the Holy See the faculty of directing disposal assets when and where it deemed necessary or suitable.

It is also understood that the above-mentioned administration will report annually to the Holy See.

The Supreme Pontiff is most grateful for Your Reverence's fervent and assiduous prayers for Him and sends to you, your fellow-workers, the hospital patients and all those who give their loving Christian assistance to this project, the requested Apostolic Blessing.

Yours most devotedly in the Lord,
Angelo Dell'Acqua
Substitute

This correspondence between Padre Pio and the Vatican took place in the early months of 1957, before the Giuffré scandal broke. How could anyone then have suspected that he had made illicit use of the money entrusted to him? How, in the Vatican itself, certainly against the Pope's wishes, could there have been manoeuvres against him? It is another of the mysteries of the stigmatic friar's life that he should have had, along with so many admirers, such bitter enemies.

Chapter 15

Padre Pio's friends

Above all, Padre Pio had friends. Naturally I am not referring to the large number of his devotees throughout the world, people who were so impressed by his charisma that they accepted his own account of his spiritual life on trust and shared in his charitable works by sending huge sums of money to support them. I am referring to 'important' friends, leading men in the Church who evidently did not believe those who denigrated the 'saint of Gargano'. Pope John XXIII himself, who for obvious reasons had to sanction Monsignor Maccari's enquiry into the administration of the House for the Relief of Suffering, was very kindly disposed towards Padre Pio, as may be seen from the following letter of 27 January 1959 written to him by Cardinal Tardini, substitute Secretary of State for His Holiness.

Very Reverend Father,
The deep filial respect that you have for the person of the Vicar of Jesus Christ was most evident in the letter you recently wrote to His Holiness giving valuable information about the promising development of the House for the Relief of Suffering.
His Holiness was well satisfied and most happy to receive such good and encouraging news from Your Reverence about an institution which is so dear to your heart.
If indeed every generous work and every noble enterprise of the children of God cannot but console the Holy Father and so deserve his high praise, this is above all the case in a work such as yours which is so imbued with the spirit of evangelical charity.
The Supreme Pontiff desires me to convey to you his warm congratulations and he is certain that the work you describe, started in the Lord's vineyard by the indefatigable zeal of one of his ministers and proceeding in the orderly fashion dictated by your way of life, will give some small glory to God and will result in an abundant supernatural harvest among souls.

After such a promising start, His Holiness most willingly sends the requested Apostolic Blessing to you, to your worthy fellow-workers, directors, doctors and assistants and especially to the patients of the House; may the Most High pour his most abundant blessings on you all.

I am happy to take this opportunity of assuring Your Reverence of my religious respect,

Yours most devotedly in the Lord,

D. Card. Tardini

The following year, Padre Pio was the centre of much polemic and his transfer to the Vatican or even to Spain was being mooted; as he approached the fiftieth anniversary of his ordination to the priesthood, Cardinal Giovanni Battista Montini, Archbishop of Milan and future Pope Paul VI, wrote as follows to the friar on 20 June 1960:

Most Venerable Father,

I have heard that Your Reverence will soon be celebrating the fiftieth anniversary of your ordination to the priesthood, so I too make bold to offer you my congratulations in the Lord on the abundant graces you have both received from God and have dispensed to the faithful. It is fitting to repeat, with joy and thanksgiving for the goodness of God, 'Come, listen, all who fear God, and I will tell you the things he has done for my soul!' That is how any priest ought to celebrate an occasion like this. How much more, then, in your case where the ministry has been blessed with so many gifts and such fruitfulness!

I also pray that Christ the Lord may live and work through you and your ministry as St Paul says, 'May the life of Jesus be manifested in our mortal bodies.'

I know that you pray for me. I need it very much; please continue to pray both for this diocese and for yours most devotedly in Christ Jesus,

G. B. Card. Montini

One can easily guess that these greetings, for an anniversary which was still fairly distant (it fell on 10 August) were merely a pretext for letting Padre Pio know that Cardinal Montini had no part in the 'conspiracy' against the friar, which was brewing at that time. In fact, Cardinal Montini was to say to Monsignor Giuseppe Del Ton, 'If they don't want Padre Pio at San Giovanni Rotondo, I'll have him here. He could celebrate at the cathedral and his Mass would do Milan more good than a mission.'

A few days later, on 2 July, Archbishop Marco Castellano, assistant chaplain general of Catholic Action, also sent his congratulations to Padre Pio:

> Very Reverend Father,
> Italian Catholic Action would like to be remembered at your jubilee Mass and have asked me to convey their warmest congratulations and best wishes to you.
> Many of our members and directors have received great spiritual consolation and a new impetus in their apostolate from your priestly ministry and you have prayed constantly that Catholic Action might continue to flourish and to fulfil its most delicate and noble mission. For all this we give you a big 'thank you' and wish you 'many happy returns!'
> With my deep respect, may the Lord bless you abundantly,
> Yours most devotedly
> Marco Castellano

Greetings also came from the United States, from the Archbishop of Chicago:

> Dear Padre Pio,
> With feelings of true spiritual affection, I would like to assure you of my warmest congratulations and heartfelt joy on the solemn occasion of your golden jubilee on 10 August.
> As I wrote to Padre Domenico, my Mass on 9 August will be offered for your intentions, in special thanksgiving for all the Lord's graces during these fifty years. I have often felt during my life how the visits I have been privileged to make to San Giovanni Rotondo have helped me in my work as bishop. May I ask you once more to pray for me?
> With a very special blessing for you and once again my warmest wishes,
> I remain yours very affectionately in Our Lord,
> Albert Cardinal Meyer

This was a time when Padre Pio's enemies were particularly active so, as well as the good wishes, it was not surprising to read the following lines from Cardinal Lercaro, who had already expressed his devotion to the stigmatic friar on several occasions, defending him against those who tried to challenge the integrity of his charitable works:

In this world, the redemption does not rid us of suffering, rather it places suffering within the divine plan as a sharing in the cross of Christ. In paradise, certainly, 'there will be no more pain or struggle or tears', as there will be no shadow of sin.

But already here below suffering is illuminated by hope; it is accompanied by that intimate peace of heart which trustingly accepts the ever-benevolent will of God; the sufferer is consoled by the certainty that pain is not merely a useless and hopeless misfortune but, united to the Heart of Jesus, it becomes expiation, purification, an instrument of personal sanctification and a guarantee of love for the Lord, an irresistible power of intercession.

What is more, when we have the spirit of Jesus, suffering is alleviated by charity; Christ is specially present in our suffering brothers and sisters and when we give them our compassionate care and generous service in an attempt to take the weight of their cross, we minister to Christ himself.

So, if we can never have an earthly paradise here below, we can find blessed oases where suffering transfigured by hope encounters that charity which is a heavenly virtue. This is only possible through the Redemption wrought by Christ in the Church and through the Church which carries on his mission . . . The more deeply we live in the spirit of Christ's teaching and his cross, the more we shall be able to create such 'oases'.

At San Giovanni Rotondo, in the light of the crucified Saviour, the marks of whose passion are mysteriously present in Padre Pio, there has for a long time been solid teaching on the demands of the Gospel. Hidden at first, this teaching finally took flesh in a House for the Relief of Suffering which has now been enlarged and fully equipped; a wonderful oasis where the Christian spirit permeates all the resources of science and technology in order to bring comfort not only to the body but also to the heart and soul. The light of faith and power of grace descending on souls in the confessional has turned many a soul in a new direction and inflamed many a heart with charity . . . and charity 'non agit perperam'.

So Padre Pio, having led innumerable souls to repentance, turns, on this his jubilee day, like Jesus, to those who suffer and repeats the divine words to them, 'Come, all who are burdened and oppressed and you will find refreshment for your souls . . .' In the big house at San Giovanni Rotondo there is not only the latest scientific equipment: there is also the heart and spirit of Jesus.

G. Card. Lercaro

Even the political world sent messages of esteem and sincere good wishes to Padre Pio on the fiftieth anniversary of his ordination.

Here are a few of them:

Padre Pio's good works are known throughout the world. They are associated not only with the wonderful and happily inspired hospital centre of San Giovanni Rotondo but also with the spiritual joy and inner renewal experienced by all who have had the good fortune to meet him and see him for themselves.

Guido Gonella
Minister of State

It is an agreeable duty to send my good wishes to the venerable Father who, with his work and prayer, draws attention to the presence of Franciscan charity in our tormented and troubled world.

Giulio Andreotti
Minister of State

My deep gratitude for your witness as a Franciscan, for the suffering you bear for the good of all, for the sincerity with which you so courageously consent to share the Lord's Passion. We all hope you will remain among us to recall us to a more consistent and more Christian life-style, bringing us the perpetual blessings of peace and divine goodness.

Luigi Scalfaro
Minister of State

Your magnificent and noble acts of fraternal charity on behalf of both physical and spiritual sufferers, surely bear significant witness to the power of Christian virtue in the service of humanity, both now and in the future.

Antonio Segni
President of the Republic of Italy

Chapter 16

A disconcerting friend:
Emanuele Brunatto

Emanuele Brunatto, a most faithful friend of Padre Pio, was always ready to defend the friar's work. In 1927 he collaborated with Monsignor Felice Bevilacqua in the inquiry which led to the demotion of Archbishop Gagliardi of Manfredonia who had fiercely and unjustly accused the stigmatic friar. And again in 1960 he assisted Monsignor Maccari in his inquiry into the use of the money sent to the House for the Relief of Suffering. Who was Emanuele Brunatto?

One could describe him as a bizarre character, a sort of cross between an angel and a devil. Certainly in his youth he was predominantly evil: a dedicated *bon viveur*, a dancer at the Turin *café concert* in the years immediately preceding the *belle époque*, a tailor, in many ways a dyed-in-the-wool sceptic; a gourmet, he described himself as 'a great lover and a libertine.'

He was born in 1892. At the age of thirty, he suddenly underwent a mystical experience and, having heard about Padre Pio, he decided to move to San Giovanni Rotondo. He was delighted to meet the stigmatic friar and became his most faithful lay follower, to the point of taking up permanent residence at the friary of San Giovanni Rotondo.

In 1923 the persecution of Padre Pio reached its height: the Archbishop of Manfredonia forbade the friary to receive 'fanatics and enthusiasts', that is, all the followers of the friar, who believed in his holiness. The friars were forced to turn Emanuele Brunatto out; he yelled and screamed, protesting that he did not wish to leave the friary. Just outside the friary was a small shed which served as a hen-house. Emanuele Brunatto had a bright idea: 'This is not the friary,' he said and went in, scattering the frightened hens as he did so.

The friars, nonplussed, called Padre Pio to come and see.

A wild-eyed, furious Brunatto was standing at the far end of the hen-house. He looked so comical that Padre Pio could not help laughing. 'So you've become a friar now, have you, or rather a hermit?' he said but he did not send him away.

Emanuele Brunatto lived in that hen-house for three years; the floor space was three by four metres so both he and the hens were rather uncomfortable. He emerged at intervals from his lair but only to see what was going on round Padre Pio whose rare visits he enjoyed.

Meanwhile Padre Pio was being subjected to a flood of abuse from the bishopric of Manfredonia. Brunatto unearthed a whole pile of written evidence against the very priests who were criticizing the friar: corruption, vendettas, swindles. His own experience of life enabled him to detect all these squalid activities which he faithfully recorded for posterity in several dossiers. It was thanks to his labours that Monsignor Bevilacqua was able to reach the conclusion that there was not a word of truth in Monsignor Gagliardi's accusations.

Then Brunatto disappeared completely. Some in San Giovanni Rotondo believed he had emigrated, to France, it was said. Years went by. One day Padre Pio received a cheque for three-and-a-half million French francs, an astonishing sum for that time. Who but Brunatto could have sent it? It was indeed Brunatto. Having emigrated to France, he had made his fortune: he had taken over a company which ran the French railways. The pleasure-seeker of Turin, the mystic of Gargano, had now become a French financier who had not forgotten Padre Pio and had sent him that gift.

But the restless libertine in Emanuele Brunatto had once more come to the fore. He remained abstemious only in the matter of food but for the rest he resumed his riotous lifestyle. This did not stop him, however, from rushing to San Giovanni Rotondo when Padre Pio fell under suspicion of misappropriating funds received from the faithful; it was Brunatto who sought to demonstrate the absurdity of such accusations. And when the administration of the House for the Relief of Suffering was taken out of Padre Pio's hands, it was Brunatto who leapt to the friar's defence by preparing a white paper to be sent to the United Nations, no less. In a letter of 29 October 1960 addressed to the Vatican

Secretary of State he expressed his contempt for the decision which had been made. He wrote:

On 3 June 1941, through the Paris branch of the Banque Italo-Francaise de Crédit, I credited the account of the Construction Committee of the San Giovanni Rotondo Clinic at the Credito Italiano in Florence with the sum of three million, five hundred thousand French francs, equivalent to nearly three hundred million lire.

This was the very first donation received by that Committee — which had been created for the purpose — and marked the beginning of the work at San Giovanni Rotondo. As the first donor, therefore, I have a right to concern myself with this matter.

The purpose behind the Committee and the reason for my donation were the same: 'to make a donation to Padre Pio's welfare work in the place of his residence.' And that was the reason for the donations which followed. Now it is important to point out that in my case, as in others known to me, it was a question of donations made in a spirit of reparation and thus sacred and inalienable, sent for exclusive administration by Padre Pio so that he might use them in the spirit in which they were sent, for his work in the House for the Relief of Suffering.

So anyone, however important he might be, would be guilty of high-handed, immoral, illegal simony if he presumed to take over the mandate that the founders and subscribers to the work have conferred on Padre Pio and on him alone.

The Capuchin authorities bore witness to this when they conferred on Padre Pio the autonomy necessary to set up and direct this project. In his turn, Pius XII of sacred memory gave his sanction to this autonomy by dispensing Padre Pio from the vow of poverty.

This was not a sudden decision on the part of the Pope. In 1956, in an audience given to the cardiologists who took part in the congress at San Giovanni Rotondo, the Holy Father declared:

'The hospital of San Giovanni Rotondo which is now opening its doors for the first time, is the fruit of deep intuition, the outcome of an ideal matured and perfected by constant contact with the most varied and cruel aspects of human suffering, both moral and physical.'

In his turn, His Eminence Cardinal Lercaro who opened the House on 5 May 1956 concluded his speech thus:

'Where God is, there is charity and love . . . have you been aware of this at San Giovanni Rotondo? Yes, everyone has been aware of it: God is here; so of course charity and love are here. Now Padre Pio will speak to you about it.'

Finally, in July 1959, His Eminence Cardinal Tedeschini opened the Church of Our Lady of Grace which was attached to San Giovanni Rotondo and conveyed to the bedridden Padre Pio the best wishes and blessing of His Holiness Pope John XXIII.

But, hardly a year later, an apostolic visitation was to reverse the position of the Holy See, placing Padre Pio *sub judice* and setting up an inquiry into his work. This inquiry was biased against Padre Pio and subjected his activities to the brutal glare of publicity. In his frequent speeches, the Visitor not only revealed the motives and aims of his investigation but he also prejudiced the outcome by giving it to be understood that the Holy See was determined to change the structures of the House for the Relief of Suffering so that direct responsibility would be taken out of the hands of those to whom Padre Pio had entrusted it . . . which amounted to the expropriation of the work, thus violating the wishes of the founders and donors and denying the right of ownership which had been granted to Padre Pio both by the Holy See and by Italian law. And all this to bring about the downfall of the House for the Relief of Suffering to which no one would donate another penny if it were not for Padre Pio!

But that was not enough. For the first time ever, the Apostolic Visitor held a press conference about his visitation which was reported by numerous Italian and foreign newspapers. His statements were more or less exaggerated, amplified or distorted according to the varying religious views of the correspondents. In any case all of them exploited the official capacity of their informant and reported the doubts expressed by him as to the capabilities or honesty of Padre Pio's helpers and hence the sound judgement of the Padre Pio himself. And because one cannot lack good judgement and be a saint at the same time, certain journalists thereby deduced that people were quite free to doubt Padre Pio's sanctity and therefore the supernatural nature of his

69

stigmata and other extraordinary manifestations. Some newspapers came to the logical conclusion that it was a question of morbid phenomena or culpable fraud . . . which moved them to describe the technical details and give their readers a 'scientific' explanation.

Predictably, this systematic defamation spread all over the world in a matter of days, blackening the name of Padre Pio, his fellow-workers, his work, the Capuchin order and finally the Church. At the same time, the Secretariat of State was instructing the Catholic press to keep silent about Padre Pio, thus giving their tacit consent to the spirit if not the letter of the Apostolic Visitor's pronouncements, both official and unofficial.

The damage was done and it was enormous. Fifty years of priestly witness, of incessant physical and mental suffering, gallons of blood shed (ten times the weight of a man!), the balanced, loving and intelligent service given to the Church, thousands of miracles and innumerable conversions . . . all this was called in question, denigrated, twisted, by a nobody who claimed to speak in the name of the Supreme Pontiff and who in any case acted under the orders or with the consent or acquiescence of certain church authorities not least of whom was this same Secretariat.

The damage has been done and it must be repaired. It remains to be seen if we shall be able to repair it — as I wish to with all my heart — with or without the help of, or maybe even in spite of the Secretariat of State.

So that they may come to a conscientious decision in this matter, I am placing at the disposal of the Secretariat the outline of a book describing the historic mission of Padre Pio in relation to the Catholic Church, supported by completely reliable and exclusive documentation.

I am not making any demands; I am merely supplying essential evidence for forming a judgement of Padre Pio and his work; I am making no threats to anyone but I am ready and determined — as are all my friends — to disrupt this diabolical plot which has been going on for a third of a century, if Padre Pio's liberty is restricted or if there is the slightest modification in the structure of his work without his permission or ours.

On the feast of the Immaculate Conception,

E. Brunatto

In spite of Emanuele Brunatto's vigorous defence, Padre Pio was to be subjected to humiliations and restrictions for some time longer and only in 1964 would he be definitely authorized to resume all his priestly duties and his good works in the service of humanity.

Chapter 17
Mary Pyle

It was a cold January day in 1923 when the coach from Foggia drove into San Giovanni Rotondo: a battered old vehicle which only just managed to cover the forty kilometres in two hours, along a stony road full of potholes. It stopped in the main square where there was the usual group of country-folk waiting to stare at the foreigners who came to meet Padre Pio. That day, a beautiful lady stepped down from the coach; tall and blonde, she wore city clothes and asked for Padre Pio in broken Italian. A peasant offered to take her to the friary. When they got there, the lady was struck by the poverty of the building and by the wild countryside around. She looked around and went into the small church, covering her head with a multicoloured scarf. The church was empty, except for a friar with bandaged hands kneeling in front of the high altar. The lady, deeply moved, walked slowly up to him and called out, 'Padre Pio, Padre Pio!' But the friar did not answer and did not move; he went on praying, his eyes fixed on the crucifix. The stranger took courage and tried to shake him gently. Padre Pio turned round and said in a tone of reproof, 'What do you want? Let me pray to the Lord in peace.'

That was Mary Pyle's first encounter with Padre Pio: an encounter which made a deep impression on her and determined the course of her life. Padre Pio's brusque manners, which concealed a great kindness, won the heart of the foreigner who, a few days later, decided to give up all her wealth and her most precious possessions in order to dedicate herself to the stigmatic friar, living close to the friary and sustaining her soul with prayer.

Born in New York in 1888 into a very rich family of soap manufacturers, Mary Pyle had always lived in the lap of luxury. She was a lovely girl with many boyfriends; one day she fell seriously in love but her parents were not happy with the man she had chosen. So Mary Pyle was sent to Italy 'to forget'. The First World War was scarcely over. The beautiful American girl began a teacher-training course with Maria Montessori but her spirits sank from day to day as she sadly missed her boyfriend who was still writing to her.

One day, telling her troubles to a friend, she heard about the humble young friar with the stigmata who comforted the afflicted and, it was said, also worked miracles. The unhappy American girl decided then and there to go to San Giovanni Rotondo to make her confession to him but many days were to elapse between the first time when she saw Padre Pio wrapped in prayer in church and her actual confession. Padre Pio continually turned her roughly away, refusing to absolve her and so forcing her to stay on in San Giovanni Rotondo. The friar sensed that the foreigner had come to him because of a particular state of soul and that she needed to be shaken out of her spiritual torpor. His refusal to absolve her disturbed Mary and drew her even more strongly to the friar, who finally heard her confession.

The day after receiving communion, Mary met Padre Pio in the little kitchen garden of the friary while the friars were busy tending the flowerbeds.

'Why did you leave America, to see the war damage in Italy?' said the friar, staring at her intently. Mary answered,

'I came to Italy to study.'

'And to forget!' added the friar mischievously.

'Yes, Father, for that, too; but since I've been at San Giovanni Rotondo I haven't wanted to go back to America. I want to stay here with you and learn to pray to the Lord.'

From then on, every morning at four o'clock Mary slipped out along the dusty path to the friary to hear Mass and receive communion from Padre Pio.

Having decided not to go home again, the girl informed her parents in a letter in which, among other things she said, 'My dear parents, now I am really happy. Living in this remote but delightful little village in Puglia, I have discovered that there is another sort of life which is worth living, with no worries and anxieties. I have discovered that more than the body it is the spirit that needs nourishment and nothing nourishes it more than prayer. Living here in a cold little friary as a follower of the Little Poor Man of Assisi; his name is Padre Pio and he has the stigmata in his hands and feet. Every morning he celebrates Mass before dawn when the country-folk are going off to work in the fields. His whole daily life is an example of humility and dedication to the Lord. He despises worldly goods, putting supreme value on Christ's love alone. I feel I've always lived here among these gentle people; I feel I was born here. I miss you – it's the only thing that makes me sad – but I pray for you. I don't know what to do with my belongings; only, I'd like to help those who suffer and are hungry and naked.'

Quite desperate, Mary's parents rushed over to Italy and tried to persuade the girl to go back to the United States. But all attempts failed: the girl's father and mother returned to America disappointed and decided not to send her any more money. So the daughter of the 'soap king' of New York was practically reduced to living off alms just so that she could be near Padre Pio. The problem was soon solved, however; all sorts of help began to come from the United States and in the end even her parents fell into the habit of sending her some percentage of the family income which Mary then passed on to those in need.

One day Padre Pio said to the American benefactress, 'We need a new organist for the old organ in our church; would you feel like playing it?' Pleasantly surprised, she answered, 'I can't play, Father, but I'd be happy to learn the organ in order to serve the Lord a bit more.' So it was that Mary became Padre Pio's organist.

Although she was very wealthy, she lived in poverty, giving her money to good works. Thanks to her a friary was built where about ninety young friars were housed as well as the first helpers at the House for the Relief of Suffering. She was one of the first people to learn of Padre Pio's desire to build this House, when one day he looked at the bare hillside opposite the friary and said to her, 'I'd like to see a hospital built on that rock through the goodwill of all, a hospital for the poor; for those who suffer in their bodies and have no chance of relieving their suffering.' And Mary answered, 'Father, it's enough that you want it.'

After that, in order to be nearer the friary and to the place where the hospital was to be built, Mary had a small villa built for her nearby where she was always happy to welcome the faithful who came from all over the world to visit the stigmatic friar. Her favourite guests were certainly 'Aunt Giuseppa' and 'Uncle Orazio', Padre Pio's parents, who came to San Giovanni Rotondo in 1928 and were lovingly helped by her. Both of them died in the arms of the 'little American' who sought to comfort them and relieve their pain until the end.

She died a few months before Padre Pio in May 1968. All the brothers from the Friary of Our Lady of Grace were at her funeral. Only Padre Pio was absent. While the brothers stood round the humble bier in the church adjoining the friary, listening, deeply moved, to the funeral oration of Father Carmelo, the guardian, Padre Pio prayed alone in his cell. When a friar told him that Mary had suffered a cerebral thrombosis and was in a coma, Padre Pio had seemed stunned with grief but he had not wanted to go to see her. 'I will pray the Lord to receive her into paradise with the angels,' he answered and after a few moments added, 'At last she'll be able to listen to the celestial melodies without having to play them.'

He had last met Mary, now a tired and white-haired old lady, two days before she died when she had received communion in the new friary church for the last time. Then she had knelt before Padre Pio and kissed his hand, just as on that far-off day in 1923 when she had received absolution and had chosen the way she would live and die.

Chapter 18

The disappearance of the 'engineer'

In contrast to Mary Pyle who had the friars of Our Lady of Grace close at hand when she died, and the prayers of Padre Pio, Angelo Lupi died in 1969 forgotten by all. Who was he? The 'engineer' of the House for the Relief of Suffering, or rather the humble surveyor to whom Padre Pio had entrusted the task of building the hospital.

He had already been forgotten by everyone for some time. So forgotten that when Padre Pio died, he was forbidden to go up to his cell. And when journalists from all over the world came pouring into the little Gargano village to find out about the life and works of Padre Pio just after his death, no one remembered Angelo Lupi, the man whom the 'saint of San Giovanni' called 'Engineer' and who had been his right-hand man in the construction of the hospital.

He died alone in his native village near Pescara on the Adriatic coast, his rosary in his hands, and a photograph of the smiling Padre Pio on his bedside table. The man who had battled with real engineers and technicians to build, brick by brick, the hospital which was to be the focal point of Padre Pio's life, who had suffered the hostility of those who did not believe in his ability as a builder, died with the great desire to visit Padre Pio's tomb for the last time. A few days before his death, turning to a member of his family he said, with tears in his eyes, 'I would like to see San Giovanni Rotondo for the last time and to visit Padre Pio's tomb . . .' Perhaps he was remembering that far-off evening when Padre Pio, having called him into his cell, confided to him the idea of building a great hospital for the poor on the bare hillside and asked him to take charge of the construction himself. That evening, Angelo Lupi became a '*de facto* engineer'. He set out with intelligence, skill and above all faith, to build the complex which would excite worldwide admiration and would amaze the professional engineers with all their degrees and academic qualifications.

Chapter 19

Padre Pio's long day

Padre Pio's day was always the same: he spent it in constant communion with the Lord in prayer. It started at half past two while it was still dark; summer and winter, with no regard to the outdoor temperature which was almost the same as in the miserable little cell. When one day they decided to install a radiator in the friar's cell to warm it up in the icy winter weather, he opposed it with all his might and succeeded in preventing anyone from starting the job.

Hardly had he risen from his bed, or rather his miserable cot, than Padre Pio started praying in preparation for his celebration of Mass which began punctually at four o'clock. At his express wish Mass was usually celebrated out of doors – weather permitting – so that the local peasants who went to work at dawn could be present.

He was very fond of the peasants; it could hardly have been otherwise as he came from the same background himself. 'Oh how I love the peasants,' he once exclaimed, 'I feel such affinity with them; and how I wish that the sweat they pour into the dry furrows could be transformed into thanksgiving to the Lord!' He loved the people of the land and was happy to celebrate the sacrifice of the Mass for them as dawn broke.

Actually, ever since he had been in Pietrelcina as a young friar the peasants had not been too happy with his preference for them because Padre Pio's Mass was long: it lasted more than an hour and they liked to get to the fields before sunrise. But if at first they grumbled they slowly began to come in great numbers and the service filled them with such joy that they were able to face their hard work in the fields with greater serenity.

I often went to Padre Pio's Mass. I tried to watch every movement of his hands and eyes but at the same time I was fascinated by the way he celebrated the rite as a whole. I remember that the elevation of the host was the most beautiful and moving moment. The minutes went by in the most profound and mystical silence while the friar lifted up the white host. And he remained like that, his arms raised as if begging for grace, and his eyes fixed on the host, his face would light up, his eyes would grow wider and begin to shine as if filled with tears, while his lips moved in prayer. It was as if Padre Pio were in ecstasy: he would gaze so intently at the host that it seemed as if he were speaking to it, his face tense, his body trembling. Only at these rare moments − at the elevation of the host − was it possible to look at Padre Pio's eyes; otherwise, it was impossible to sustain his gaze. Once I timed the elevation of the host at Padre Pio's Mass: exactly twenty minutes. But although it was such a long Mass, the faithful would stay on in their places for several hours, so deeply were they affected.

On 23 May 1987 in the Shrine of Our Lady of Grace at San Giovanni Rotondo, on the occasion of his visit to celebrate the centenary of the friar's birth, Pope John Paul II spoke of Padre Pio's Mass: 'Who does not remember the fervour with which Padre Pio relived the passion of Christ in the Mass? That is why he held the Mass in such high esteem, calling it the "great mystery", the decisive moment of salvation and sanctification for humankind through sharing in the very sufferings of Christ crucified. The Mass was the pivot and centre of his whole life and work. Out of this intimate and loving participation in the sacrifice of Christ, sprang his dedicated service of souls, especially those caught up in sin and in the miseries of life.'

The best and most eloquent testimony to the value of Padre Pio's lengthy Mass is the fact that thousands and thousands of people from all over the world would stay on their knees for an hour in order to be present at the most sublime mystery of our religion.

But let us return to his day. When Mass was over, the friar of San Giovanni would go back to his cell where he would drink a cup of coffee. Then at six o'clock he would shut himself into his confessional to receive sinners and give them God's forgiveness.

At twelve o'clock the stigmatic friar would recite the Angelus with the faithful and then bless them. Immediately after that, he would join the other friars in the common refectory and take up his place which was on the left on entering. Padre Pio's lunch consisted of a spoonful of soup or a few vegetables and half a glass of wine. When his fellow friars urged him to eat, he would say, 'But I've had enough; my stomach feels full.' Then they would jokingly say, 'Padre Pio lives on air.'

In 1967 Cardinal Bacci was a guest at the friary, having been sent by the Vatican to find out about Padre Pio's lifestyle. In the refectory the cardinal, noticing that the friar was not eating, said in gentle reproof,

'Padre Pio, why aren't you eating with us?'

'Your Eminence, I'm not hungry!'

'Out of obedience to your monastic rule you should eat something!'

At these words, Padre Pio lowered his eyes, picked up his fork and went through the motions of eating. The cardinal who had not taken his eyes off the friar, smiled and said,

'But Padre Pio, you're deceiving me, you're just pretending to eat!'

'Forgive me, Your Eminence, but my stomach is full!'

'Oh well, this time I'll forgive you,' the cardinal said good-naturedly.

He was never once greedy, never did he do justice to the monastic menu! The sole exception to this rigorous fast, as well as practically his only food, was his morning cup of coffee which he drank partly because of his heart condition. Even the local doctors could not give a 'scientific' explanation for the fact that the friar lived without any food. Padre Pio said of himself, 'Satisfying bodily needs such as eating, drinking and sleeping are such a torment to me that I can only compare it with the pains suffered by the martyrs when they made the supreme sacrifice. Don't think I'm exaggerating! No! It really *is* like that!'

After his 'mock meal', Padre Pio went back to his cell to pray. At about three o'clock he went down to the church to hear more confessions until five o'clock when he allowed himself a short rest: in the summer in the courtyard of the friary, in the winter on the verandah. He would talk with the other friars and with a few of the faithful. He would relax like this for half an hour and then would go to the

House for the Relief of Suffering and talk to the doctors, directors and administrators. Then he went back to his cell again, first of all to recite more rosaries, then, at seven o'clock, to appear at the little window to bless the faithful who would gather below in great numbers every day. At half past seven he would go down to the refectory for supper and immediately afterwards to his cell where he prayed until his eyes closed and his lips stopped moving during one of the *Ave Maria* which he would recite by the hour.

That was Padre Pio's day, always the same, always full of prayer, suffering, renunciation, words of comfort for the suffering and smiles for those who rejoiced in the name of the Lord.

Chapter 20

Friendly rebukes

I have written a great deal about Padre Pio but when I had to write about his illness or the lack of understanding of him as a person, I always found it a distressing task. To me it was a professional duty but also a religious one because I wanted to draw people's attention to him and to keep his many friends throughout Italy informed of his activities. But my articles sometimes earned an affectionate rebuke. I remember a meeting with him in the early days of 1966.

As I stepped over the friary threshold I was feeling worried. Not about the rebuke, of course, as I could hardly have foreseen that, but because I had with me the photographer Lo Muzio of Foggia and the idea was not only to interview the 'saint of Gargano' but also to take several photographs of him. And I knew very well that he did not like being interviewed, still less photographed. Scarcely had I entered the friary when I caught a glimpse of him but I could see at once how tired he was: every step was an effort, every handshake caused him pain and made him grimace. Padre Pio certainly seemed to have aged, even taking into account that it was Friday, the day on which for years he had suffered more intensely from his stigmata. Those wounds, in fact, would bleed more copiously on that day of the week as if to renew the pain of Christ on the day of his passion.

'I would like to suffer more, I wish the Lord would grant me the joy of feeling the pain at every moment of my life,' the stigmatic friar would say to the confrères who supported him on either side as he celebrated Mass and tried to spare him the least exertion. But Padre Pio would not stop, he would not give in, he seemed determined to defy the doctors and to take no account of his age and his poor health in order to be as faithful as possible to his task of prayer and listening to people's troubles. He would have liked to say Mass every day before dawn regardless of the weather, as he had done

81

for so many years: come rain or shine, the Lord must always be served, nothing can stop one from praying. But by that time these things were no longer possible. He even had to say Mass less often. Two friars would accompany him to the altar supporting him and at times almost holding him upright; and he suffered from these limitations. One morning when they saw him weeping quietly in his cell as he fingered his rosary beads, they asked him, 'Padre Pio, why are you weeping?' And he answered through his sobs, 'You won't let me serve the Lord any more.'

Prayer, however, remained his daily bread and constant sustenance. He would pray quietly even during the short journey from his cell to the altar or on the stairs leading to the church. His lips were never still. Yet he had so much time for prayer, all night in fact, as for many years past he had hardly lain down on a bed. After supper he would retire to his cell and sit in the middle of his bed, leaning his back against the wall. That was his way of resting. He would stay like that for several hours until, worn out by the enormous fatigue of his day, his eyelids would close, only to open again shortly afterwards. That was all he had in the way of sleep.

Chapter 21

Fighting with the devil

It was only after much friendly persuasion on the part of his confrères and the kindly insistence of his superior that Padre Pio agreed to place a pillow between his back and the wall. He always refused himself the slightest physical comfort but he no longer wanted to be left alone. Every evening two or three friars went to his cell with him and recited a great number of rosaries with him until his voice gradually faded out and his eyes closed. At that point he was left alone, his head leaning back, his hands still holding the rosary. Why was Padre Pio afraid to be left alone? Because he was afraid of the dark? One of the friars confided to us that for several nights a deafening din had been heard in Padre Pio's cell. When the other friars had rushed to the spot they had found his belongings in incredible confusion and the friar himself in a terrible state of nerves: there were all the signs of a strenuous but unequal struggle with some unseen intruder. Perhaps that was why Padre Pio was afraid to be alone: not out of weakness or for fear of being overcome but simply because he felt so weary. Some time before we met in November, he had said to his superior, 'When will you let me die?' To which his confrère had replied, 'What are you saying? We still need you here so badly, we need your prayers.'

Padre Pio answered, 'Everyone can pray to the Lord. We can all be saved. It's enough to have faith.'

My friar friends and I were discussing these things while I waited for the requested interview. And I was very distressed to hear some of them. I was very sad to hear that Padre Pio had aged so much. Finally the appointed time came. Hardly had I entered his cell when I saw that my first impression had been correct, as had the tales I had heard. Padre Pio seemed tired and he had aged. Only his eyes were as quick and bright as ever; and his gaze made people bow their head and look at the ground. The 'saint of Gargano' was in front of the small window which looks over the garden and the courtyard of the friary. He had black rosary beads in his hands. He looked at us in astonishment and then turned to the friar who was with us:

'What do these people want with me?'

'Father,' said the friar, 'these are our friends from Rome who have come to see you.'

'What are their names?'

The friar reminded him that we had often been to see him. I went forward to kiss his hand and said:

'Father, first of all I'd like your blessing.'

'I bless you and all your family,' he said, making the sign of the cross on my forehead. And immediately afterwards:

'What do you do?'

'I'm a journalist, Father.'

'And what do you write about?'

'About what goes on around me, Father, but I particularly want to write about you.'

'About me? And what are you going to write about me?'

'Your life, your sufferings, the good you do for humanity, your miracles.'

'Miracles, eh? Miracles . . . But what are you saying? I don't perform miracles, I just pray.'

Padre Pio's voice grew hard, almost as if he were rebuking me for likening him to a saint.

'But everyone calls you "the saint of San Giovanni" ' I said. Padre Pio looked at me severely.

'Saints are only in heaven, lad.'

'Father, do you remember me now?'

'Of course I remember you, you're the one who makes me die every now and then, in the papers.'

'Not at all, Father. I've come to San Giovanni to find out about the state of your health.'

'And to write nonsense,' he interrupted, and he seemed almost angry.

'No, Father. I try to do my job properly,' I found the courage to reply.

'A fine job, telling other people's business,' he said, but this time his voice was gentler.

'The last time I came here, Father, I couldn't see you because you were ill in bed. How do you feel now?'

'Better, better; and don't worry so much about my health because the day is coming when they will carry me to say Mass in a chair', he answered mischievously, then he got up and went out of his cell, allowing himself to be supported on either side.

The photographer Lo Muzio took some photographs and Padre Pio immediately reacted in irritated fashion,

'What do you think you're playing at?'

'Father, we would like to take a few photographs of you', I put in.

'Very well, may God's will be done', he answered, heaving a deep sigh.

Then Padre Pio held out his hand for us to kiss and to dismiss us but we hesitated. And he said:

'And now what do you want? I have blessed you and I've let you take the photograph with that contraption, why don't you go away?'

'Padre Pio, tell us something to say to our readers,' I almost begged him.

'What can I tell you? . . . Pray and do good to those who suffer. Pray for the peace of the world; pray always and go to Mass. You young people especially need to be closer to the Lord.'

'But we young people don't know how to pray as they used to in the old days. It's your prayers we need.'

'What's that? Only the young need prayers? And what about the old?'

Then, turning to the photographer who was still taking photos from time to time:

'Have you finished playing with that contraption?'

Lo Muzio, coming forward and kissing his hand, murmured a few words of explanation but Padre Pio cut him short,

'So you want to spend your life taking photos of me?'

I managed to put in another question:

'Why does your Mass take so long? And at the elevation of the host why do you stand still looking at it for over a quarter of an hour?'

The friar who had come with us made a gesture of disapproval and gave me a warning look but after a moment's silence Padre Pio exclaimed:

'Hey, lad, now you want to know too much! Is there a fixed length of time for praying to the Lord?'

Finally, as we were taking our leave, I asked another question:

'Father, are you really free now?'

'No one is free on this earth,' he answered almost scanning the words as he walked away from us, his head bowed.

A smiling and relaxed Padre Pio. He shunned publicity and discouraged the curiosity of the public.

Padre Pio's father, Orazio Forgione (1859-1946).

Padre Pio's mother, Maria Giuseppe di Nunzio (1859-1929).

Right: Padre Pio's sister Grazia, who took the name Pia as a Brigidine nun.
Below: The chapel of the Invisible Stigmata near Pietrelcina. It was here that in 1910 Padre Pio experienced for the first time the pains in his hands and feet. The visible marks appeared much later, when he was in the monastery at San Giovanni Rotondo, on 20 September 1918.

Left: The young Padre Pio in a distinctly Franciscan mood.
Below: The old Capuchin monastery at San Giovanni Rotondo.

Padre Pio in 1921. The stigmata were causing him much pain. In July of that year he recorded: 'My suffering now is so acute that I feel I am dying by the minute.'

A typical day for Padre Pio always began with the celebration of the mass. The stigmata on his hands are clearly visible.

Right: Padre Pio with a group
of children after their
First Communion.
Below: Padre Pio blessing
the people in the sacristy
of the new church
of Santa Maria delle Grazie.

Padre Pio in the confessional, which was practically his world for over 50 years. The ministry of reconciliation was his main mission.

The penetrating look of Padre Pio.

Padre Pio giving his blessing at the end of a mass.

Padre Pio reading a letter. Through letters he kept in touch with his numerous spiritual children.

Close-up of a tired but serene Padre Pio.

Padre Pio receives the stigmata. Painting by Salvatore Fiume (1986).

The magnificent bronze statue of Padre Pio by Francesco Messina, at
San Giovanni Rotondo.

Padre Pio loved children. He had a special predilection for their simplicity and spontaneity.

Chapter 22

The prayer groups

'Jesus, may the prayer groups become centres of light and love in the world.' So prayed Padre Pio.

Prayer was his daily bread, it was his daily hymn of thanksgiving to the Lord for the gift of life. At about the same time as he first thought of the House for the Relief of Suffering, another big project was forming in Padre Pio's heart; this, too, was the fruit of his constant contact with the Lord.

The Second World War had only just broken out, with its threat of misery and devastation. From the Chair of St Peter a great pope, Pius XII, sent out continual appeals for united prayer for the end of hostilities among the nations. In the remote village of San Giovanni the humble friar with the bandaged hands responded to the Pope's urgent plea and intensified his prayers to the point of exhaustion. But Padre Pio did not want to pray alone, he wished other people of goodwill to join him in prayer, begging God to restore order and peaceful co-existence among the nations.

One evening in 1940, while he was talking to some of the faithful, he took a handful of rosary beads out of his pocket and gave one to each of those present, 'Pray, pray to the Lord with me, because the whole world needs prayers. And each day when you feel life's loneliness more strongly, pray, pray together to the Lord, because even God needs our prayers!' With those simple words, Padre Pio's prayer groups were born; this was perhaps the most spiritual of all his good works and it began at a time when the whole world lay under the shadow of war.

Nine years had to pass before Padre Pio's prayer groups became a functional worldwide institution but the movement inspired by Padre Pio's words started to grow at once from the nucleus at San Giovanni Rotondo. The first group formed round Padre Pio himself consisted of five people, all elderly, the first who had been asked to pray the rosary. It was the first centre from which the movement spread all over the world. Everyone who left San Giovanni Rotondo, having met the stigmatic friar, would become the spiritual leader of a new prayer group. Padre Pio's aim was to create an army of praying people who would leaven the world and encourage others everywhere to try the flavour of prayer and union with God.

Padre Pio said to one of these groups, 'We must create centres of faith and love in which Christ himself is present each time they join together in prayer and eucharistic fellowship!'

Why prayer groups? Much of today's life is centred on the group or rather the 'clan'. In politics, sport and social activities, it is not the individual who works alone but many people working together, all striving for the same goal. And quite often even when there seems to be one man at work, in fact his achievement is the result of a whole series of actions. Similarly we need the work of the group in prayer so that it may be more powerful and more readily heard by God. On 5 May 1966, the tenth anniversary of the opening of the House for the Relief of Suffering, Padre Pio was to say, 'It is prayer, the united effort of all good souls, which makes the world go round, that leads to the renewal of conscience; it is prayer that upholds the House for the Relief of Suffering, comforts the afflicted, heals the sick, sanctifies labour, supports our medical staff, lends moral courage and Christian resignation to human suffering and brings God's loving blessing on every sorrow and weakness. Pray much, my children, pray always!'

Padre Pio spent 22 September 1968, his last day on earth, meeting with his prayer groups and praying with them. On that day *L'Osservatore Romano* wrote: 'At present Padre Pio has 726 prayer groups, of which 688 are in Italy, 21 in France, 8 in Australia, 6 in Switzerland, 5 in Belgium, 5 in the United States, 3 in Germany, 2 in Luxembourg, one each in the Principality of Monaco, Morocco, South Africa, Tunisia, Turkey, El Salvador and Chile. There is also an international group in Rome in the FAO. As is well known, Padre Pio da Pietrelcina started the groups which now number 68,000 members who meet at least once a month to pray together for Padre Pio's intentions. Each group has a priest approved by the diocesan bishop as its spiritual director. Of the 726 current spiritual directors, 544 are members of the diocesan clergy, 124 are from various religious orders and congregations and 58 from the Capuchin order.'

It was actually on Padre Pio's last day on earth that an international convention of prayer groups was held at San Giovanni Rotondo, as if to show the man who inspired them that they were truly active in everyday life in all corners of the earth. And Padre Pio was so moved that he said to his superior, Father Carmelo, 'I thank the Lord that he heard my humble prayer; I am happy that so many people are united with me in prayer!'

These were the joys of the humble stigmatic friar; the true joys which brought comfort to his heart when he faced mistrust and malice or when he ministered to so many troubled souls. He bled for many years from hands, feet and side; thousands and thousands of cloths were soaked with that blood and were stacked in huge cupboards in the friary before the sceptics would believe and the unbelievers and the malicious were put to silence.

Chapter 23

Padre Pio's charity
bears fruit

Thirty years after the opening of the House for the Relief of Suffering, Cardinal Agostino Casaroli preached the following homily on 4 May 1986 at San Giovanni Rotondo:

1. Thirty years ago, on 5 May 1956, the House for the Relief of Suffering first opened its doors. It is a foundation inspired by the loving and sensitive heart of Padre Pio da Pietrelcina, that tireless mystic and stigmatic who lived in this holy and grace-filled place.

It was at the same time that Padre Pio's prayer groups officially began, although they date back much further. In fact, even before 1950, those who had been fortunate enough to meet Padre Pio had begun to meet together with no fixed programme but moved by the same spirit, to pray for his intentions, impressed and inspired as they were by his persistent exhortations and eloquent example. Padre Pio in turn was already personally convinced of the absolute necessity for prayers in the fierce daily battle against evil and wanted to take his part in building up the movement of prayer so urgently requested by Pius XII from the start of his pontificate. In his first encyclical, *Summi Pontificatus* (20 October 1939), Pius XII had in fact written these dramatic words: 'This our first encyclical comes to you at a time which is in many ways a real hour of darkness when the spirits of violence, discord and bloodshed are being unleashed as never before in the midst of the human race', and he had asked for a fervent and continuous crusade of prayer. And since then, even after the end of that dreadful World War, he had continued to ask for fervent prayer, for the ever-pressing spiritual and material needs of humanity. 'Pray, pray, pray,' he had said, 'prayer is the key to God's treasury; it is the weapon we must use to fight and win in every conflict between good and evil. There is no end to the power of prayer: adoration, propitiation, petition, intercession, thanksgiving . . . (4 September 1940). He recommended assiduous prayer on the part of priests, parents, young men and women and also stressed the importance of frequent and well-made communion for the building up and strengthening of the spiritual life.

The pope's heartfelt pleas found a ready response from Padre Pio. 'Let's go to work, let's really get down to it,' he would say, 'let's be the first to respond to the Supreme Pontiff's appeal.' From the first this response took the form of prayer groups led by him and by those around him but it was not until 5 May 1966, after years of experience and consolidation, that he was able to give a precise description of the shape and aim of such groups: 'They are seedbeds of faith, centres of love in which Christ himself is present each time they come together for prayer and eucharistic fellowship under the guidance of their pastors and spiritual directors.'

Since their official institution, which we are celebrating today with such joy and thanksgiving at this international convention, the groups have spread throughout Italy and over the various continents so that during the extraordinary Holy Year of Redemption the Holy Father John Paul II was able to receive them during their great international pilgrimage. In his address to them he described their special characteristics and identity in these words, 'Your presence and your Christian task are indissolubly linked with the personality and work of Padre Pio da Pietrelcina, the humble Capuchin friar of San Giovanni Rotondo who for nearly fifty years lived out his consecrated life almost exclusively in fervent, continual daily prayer and in the ministry of reconciliation, guiding and directing thousands of the faithful who were seeking the true way of perfection and Christian holiness' (1 October 1983).

After the appeal made in August 1950 and the institution of a system of membership, the groups began to take on a definite shape; theirs was essentially a humble, discreet and hidden role within the Church.

They were firmly linked to the Church and subject to the approval of the local bishop, who would appoint a priest for their pastoral care and assistance. Their formative and apostolic aim was: 'Through communal prayer to aid the spiritual formation and growth of all the members so that each one may be an example of Christian living, charity and devotion. For prayer should be the means of raising our minds to God, singing him a hymn of love and bringing to him, as to a most loving Father, our poor spiritual and material needs. But this should enable us to shed around us the light of the Christian faith.'

So we can say that, like the great, welcoming hospital of San Giovanni Rotondo, the prayer groups, now spread worldwide, were the fruit of Padre Pio's wonderful charity. Not only did he want to relieve physical suffering but also to heal the spiritual wounds of humanity, saving souls from evil and spurring them on to holiness.

2. The prayer groups have a great task to perform in modern society with their specific character and their specific aim of bringing Padre Pio's spirituality to everyday life in the family and in society generally.

In truth it is not easy to analyze and fathom Padre Pio's personality: countless are the biographies and studies of his writings and mysticism, analyses of his behaviour and intuitions; new elements keep emerging, necessitating further and more extensive research. On the other hand we know that he himself wrote to Father Agostino da San Marco in Lamis, his spiritual director, that he was 'a mystery to himself, unable to understand himself.' It is all the more difficult for us to understand the innermost heart of one who lived so constantly on the mystical and supernatural planes. Endowed with what one could call tremendous gifts and possessing the ability to read souls, he looked at human activities from the purely superhuman and eternal points of view; usually mild and friendly, he could be somewhat brusque at times when he thought it necessary. His long life could be described as a perpetual Calvary, where he suffered, uniting himself to Christ for the salvation of souls, and the two focal points of that life were always the sacrifice of the altar and the forgiveness of sins in the confessional. As he used to say, Jesus himself had forewarned him of his mission of love and suffering, 'My son, it is in suffering that love is revealed; you will suffer acutely in your spirit and even more acutely in your body.'

92

In 1920 when he was already nailed to the cross, he wrote to Father Benedetto in these words:

'I am feeling extremely desolate. I feel afflicted and tormented, as I seem to be alone in bearing everyone's burdens. I suffer agonies, it wears me out mentally and breaks my heart to think that I am unable to bring spiritual help to those to whom Jesus sends me, and to see so many souls justifying their evil deeds.'

How often he groaned beneath the burden of sin which weighs upon the world and, fearful for his own eternal salvation, prayed for death so that he could finally reach the mysterious place of divine happiness where free will can choose nothing but good; but he accepted God's will courageously and wrote, 'I have worked and I desire to work; I have prayed and I desire to pray; I have watched and I desire to watch; I have wept and I desire to weep forever for my exiled brothers and sisters.'

On the card commemorating his first holy Mass (10 August 1910) he had written, 'Jesus – my desire and my life – today as I lift you up in awe – in a mystery of love, may I be with you the way, the truth and the life for the world – and a holy priest for you – a perfect victim.' Padre Pio can be said to have been completely faithful to this programme right to the end of his life, until his last Mass, celebrated on 22 September 1968. Everyone was keeping high festival around him but he kept sighing, 'Rather than celebrate I should run away and disappear, I feel so embarrassed.' The *Cronistoria* reports that Padre Pio was 'pale and white-faced as if he were faraway and confused' and that he was breathless as he blessed the crowd gathered by the side stairs and repeated with deep affection, 'My children, my children!' After the celebration of Mass he wanted to go to the confessional but was carried instead to his cell, exhausted and trembling. At half past ten he wanted to greet and bless the crowd which had gathered opposite the choir window in the little church. He appeared at the window, a white and pale-faced figure, waving a handkerchief and raising a hand in blessing: 'It was an apparition, a vision as if from another world.'

Padre Pio left this world, leaving to the prayer groups the responsibile task of carrying on and spreading his spirituality.

3. One of the characteristics of modern society, acclaimed by many, deplored by many others but acknowledged by all, is 'secularization'; which means that even in institutional and legal matters, no reference is made to transcendent values or to any sort of responsibility beyond the confines of this world. Not a few people see in today's world a Christian minority confronting a society which — even in countries with a long Christian tradition — is on the whole non-Christian, a society proud of its own success in the realms of science and technology, preoccupied with its own progress and well-being. Secularization is an historical phenomenon with far-reaching consequences because, by introducing new criteria for distinguishing between good and evil, it transforms and relativizes the ethical principles of human life and behaviour which have been accepted, if not always practised, for centuries in all Christian countries. Secularization is widespread and deeply entrenched in modern society and the prayer groups aim to oppose it with the spirit of the Gospel, thus working towards the reconversion of the world after the example of Padre Pio. We know well how many people who were far from the truth, a prey to doubts or indifference, opposed to the Gospel message and the teaching of the Church, have been converted by meeting Padre Pio! It was impossible to be indifferent to Padre Pio: false notions, misguided philosophies and sentiments collapsed on contact with him!

The journalist Orio Vergani who had gone to San Giovanni to interview him, wrote 'I looked at the friar I was meant to be interviewing and all my journalistic expertise, all my carefully-worded questions evaporated as I gazed at the sight before my eyes, my mind one huge question-mark; in fact I could not take my eyes off this simple peasant friar who day after day for thirty-two years had been seated on the rustic throne of his confessional, turning first to the left and then to the right as the slow file of penitents knelt in turn before him; there he was, listening to the story of the world's sins, hearing the prayers of the whole world . . .'

Another great writer who met Padre Pio was Guido Piovene. From a non-Christian background, he still retained a certain longing for the truth without, however, deciding to embrace the faith. He was particularly impressed by Padre

94

Pio's Mass which he described in these moving lines: 'It is clear that the friar relives, in body and soul, the sacrifice of Christ; it is more than a Mass, it is a dialogue with Christ, at times intense, at times more peaceful. As he relives the various events of the passion, the conflicting emotions of joy and pain are clearly reflected in his face . . . Mass is the high point of Padre Pio's day – his prime occupations are celebrating Mass, hearing confessions, praying.'

The prayer groups, following the example of Padre Pio, should be real centres of faith, spreading the truth by setting an example of Christian living and, of course, by prayer.

4. History is and always has been a battleground between good and evil. Jesus openly affirmed this when he told the parable of the wheat and the darnel. Padre Pio would allow no illusions or utopianism: 'We shall find rest only in heaven,' he wrote 'where the victor's palm awaits us. On earth we must always fight in hope and fear, provided however that hope predominates, making us constantly aware of the all-powerful God who is at our side to help us.' It is not easy to take up the daily cross of our duty, of the Christian virtues, of patience, of chastity, of charity, in order to follow the divine Master; the way is hard, the door is narrow. The prayer groups must fight bravely against evil, always showing good grain rather than darnel, never confusing others but always being absolutely faithful to the teachings of the Church. Human history is stormy, the conflicting forces inherent in human nature lead to a succession of triumphs and failures: progress is followed by regression and defeat. 'Come,' wrote Padre Pio, 'we must take heart and fight the good fight amidst the storms of life. Blessed be the winds that raise these storms for they are the same winds which will bring us to harbour . . . However beautiful Jesus may be in glory, it seems to me that he is more beautiful as he hangs on the cross . . . Even children can love Jesus in times of consolation; but to love him when he seems absent, that is the proof of a truly faithful lover.'

In the midst of the storms Padre Pio mentions, we remain calm because we know and firmly believe that nothing lies outside the ultimate designs of Providence. To the limited vision of reason, God's plan certainly is mysterious and therefore sometimes disconcerting and painfully obscure. The 'hidden God' of Isaiah and Pascal can sometimes be a cause of anguish to us: we cannot clearly understand the ultimate motives underlying his plan; all we can see are the constant vicissitudes of human history. Padre Pio was well aware that he could neither penetrate nor comprehend the mystery of the Most High and hence that of divine Providence; that is why he entrusted himself with such faith and love to that Providence. As he wrote to one of his followers, 'Let us always strive to see in all the events of life the most wise ordering of divine Providence, let us adore it and determine always and in every way to conform ourselves to God's will; in this way we shall glorify the heavenly Father.' The prayer groups should live in this spirit of abandonment to the divine will: using their talents to the full as they go about their earthly tasks but also with complete trust in the presence of that Providence which never forsakes us. Let us remember the beautiful words of Alessandro Manzoni in his *Observations on Catholic morality*: 'The more human beings realize how weak, uncertain and negligible is their own strength and the more they can believe that they are not merely permitted but commanded to hope, the more they will feel moved to turn, or rather to throw themselves with joyful abandon into the arms of the one source of all strength and help, all foresights and faithfulness.'

The friends of Padre Pio ought to be convinced, as he was, that everything that happens in history serves, often in ways incomprehensible to us, to bring about the kingdom of grace which is God's will for us all . . .

5. Dear friends of Padre Pio! Through the prayer groups he is present in your dioceses, your parishes, your families, with his deep faith, his example, his spirituality. The words which Jesus spoke to the apostles, promising the Holy Spirit, apply to you, too: 'Peace I leave with you, my peace I give to you. I do not give to you as the world gives. Do not let your hearts be troubled, and do not let them be afraid' (John 14:27). 'No, don't be afraid,' said Padre Pio, 'you are journeying over the sea amid winds and waves; but remember that you are with Jesus! What have you to fear? But if fear overcomes you, shout loudly: Lord, save me! He will stretch out his hand to you: hold on tight and go on your way rejoicing!'

Walk in complete trust, bringing peace and serenity to the world as Padre Pio taught you; go forward with Mary most holy, our heavenly Mother, your rosary in hand! 'So let us strive,' said Padre Pio, 'like so many chosen souls, always to follow the Blessed Mother, always to walk close beside her, for there is no other road leading to life except the one trodden by our Mother.'

May these words of trust and exhortation go with us as we carry out our apostolate in the way of holiness!

Chapter 24

Padre Pio and his enduring love for the Church

Here is what Cardinal Giacomo Lercaro had to say on this subject when he spoke to the prayer groups on 8 December 1968 in the church of the Capuchin friars at Bologna:

It is with a deep sense of humility that I speak to you, brothers of the Capuchin order, faithful members of the prayer groups and all my other brothers and sisters here today. I am humbled by the figure of Padre Pio whose sudden yet expected death, by taking him beyond this world, has at last enabled us all, even his most obstinate adversaries, to perceive his spiritual stature.

I am not going to speak of the strange phenomena which drew the attention of the world to the humble Capuchin of the Gargano friary; the stigmata, the mysterious perfumes, the gifts of prophecy, the ability to read souls. I neither deny nor affirm the reality of all these, I submit them to the discernment and the judgement of the Church and I believe with St Paul that it is not these gifts of the Spirit which make him great, because, like all charisms, they are free gifts which the Lord distributes as he wills, they are given for the good of the spiritual body, that is, the ecclesial community, of which Christ is the head.

When we consider this outpouring of God's Spirit, we cannot but thank the divine goodness which has introduced into the mysterious realm of human souls such treasures of enlightenment, conversion and inspiration for good, such comfort and hope. We see God at work helping his servant to soften hearts, to free souls who have long been imprisoned; we also see souls rising out of their former sinfulness and spiritual sloth to impressive heights of generosity and commitment.

But as I was asked here to speak in commemoration of Padre Pio, I would like to recall your reverent attention to his greatest claim to glory which was his conformity to Christ Jesus, the only Son of God who is pleasing to the Father and who is our Master and supreme exemplar; all of Padre Pio's charismatic gifts were nothing more than a pointer towards this great truth: conformity to Christ is the central duty of the Christian. Yet so many of us are too distracted or too short-sighted to appreciate this.

In fact, as Paul affirms, God will glorify all those who, through his gracious design, are found to be conformed to the image of his Son.

The apostle Paul expressed this idea in his own vigorous way; and so powerfully did he share Christ's own sentiments that he could say that it was no longer he, Paul, but Christ who was living in him . . .

This obligation to conform to Christ led Padre Pio to a life of constant penance on which Christ set his luminous seal by permitting him to share the cross; like Paul, Padre Pio could say that he suffered with Christ, he was crucified with Christ and he always lived with Christ, making up — as Paul again says so powerfully — what was lacking to the sufferings of Christ.

I cannot give an adequate account here of Padre Pio's whole life — apparently so monotonous and uneventful — in order to demonstrate his loving conformity to Christ. I will have to confine myself to three elements which I feel it will be particularly helpful for us to remember today.

First of all, there is the spirit of prayer as the heart of the apostolate: Padre Pio is like Jesus, the man who converses with God, the man of prayer . . .

I remember my first meeting with him many years ago: I found him in the little choir of the old Church of Our Lady of Grace at his place of prayer. I was so pleased, even though it meant waiting to speak to him; for obviously I did not wish to take him away from his conversation with God; it seemed to me fitting to find him at prayer like that; the crowded pre-dawn Mass where he yet remained so recollected and so absorbed in prayer and the silent meditation in the empty little choir were in fact the source of that supernatural strength which was so evident in his speech — sometimes illuminating, sometimes abrupt or even harsh, but often persuasive and consoling . . .

Padre Pio had so profound a sense of the superhuman power of prayer that he wanted to help his spiritual children to pray. These children daily increased in number and he wanted to leave them this precious heritage, he wanted them to share his own longing for the coming of God's kingdom in the world and in individual souls.

So the prayer groups came into being and there his spiritual children could meet at intervals to pray and meditate together on the almighty power of our God who alone works miracles of grace in this world.

It is surprising — and it would be incomprehensible for us today if the Gospel had not warned us about humanity's lack of understanding — that the prayer groups should have encountered such difficulties and hostility precisely in the place where they could reasonably have looked for promotion and encouragement.

Yet if one really looks into the question, it was the Lord Jesus himself who encouraged them when he said that where two or three were gathered in his name he would be in the midst of them and whatever they asked the Father would be given to them . . .

But the saddest and most surprising thing of all is that this call to return to the light and strength of God should be ignored precisely by those who, according to Isaiah's image, are meant to act as 'nightwatchmen in the temple of the Lord'. Ours is indeed a dark world where secularization has made people deny or ignore the existence of God. The vertical or Godward element in human structures is totally lacking and there is no hope beyond the confines of this world; and as we survey the world scene we see, despite the wealth of scientific research and advanced technology, a devastating picture of war damage, horrific famine, destruction, division, hatred and violence . . .

In a world such as this, the members of our prayer groups proclaim the Gospel message that humanity needs God; it needs the security and hope that he gives, it needs his grace and salvation in this world and beyond. The groups bear collective witness to the salvation offered us by a loving heavenly Father and at the same time they link their members in a family which reaches out to every kind of misery, poverty and suffering. The first disciples 'persevering in prayer and in the breaking of bread, were bound together and guided by the teaching of the Apostles, being of one heart and one mind' so that — and the inspired author points out the social implications of such a life-style — 'there was not one needy person among them.'

On the eve of his death, Padre Pio who had always supported the groups by his own silent prayer saw them finally approved by the highest authorities; so amid the ranks of prayer warriors, he finished his earthly mission; in reality his life had been a continuous prayer, a constant supplication, with Christ, in Christ and through Christ, as he brought before the Father the needs and sorrows, hopes and fears of the Church and of the world . . . In his priesthood, the intercession of the one Mediator was united to the ceaseless offering which joined him to the victim of the altar; and not only round the altar of his own humble shrine but also all over the world, souls came together at his invitation and joined their prayerful supplications to the all-powerful prayer of Christ.

But Padre Pio shared in a very special way in the poverty of the Christ who became poor and naked for us in the manger and on the cross; Christ the exile, poorest of artisans in the poorest of villages; journeying hungry and homeless along the roads of the poor and needy country which he had chosen as the scene of his labours . . .

Like Christ Padre Pio was poor through his profession of poverty in an order which, in its beginnings and through successive reforms, was effectively poor. He was poor because his Capuchin life was lived out in a cell in a humble friary in the south of Italy; he never went out to broaden his horizons; his was the poverty of former times when the poor had never seen the city, never known the thrill of a journey or the delights of an excursion . . .

Padre Pio could not say with Jesus, 'foxes have holes, and birds of the air have nests; but the Son of Man has nowhere to lay his head.' In the little Friary of Our Lady of Grace he had a cell, a bed and a pillow but he did not sit down to speak on a hillside covered with anemones, nor did he climb a mountain or cross the lake where the winds ruffled the waters or whipped them into a storm . . . His was indeed a small and limited world, and sometimes in moments of extreme persecution his world was as restricted as that of a prisoner, if one could call him that. His was sometimes the life of the poorest of all, those who don't even have air, which even the birds and flowers enjoy . . . Like Christ in fact he too made himself poor in order to make others rich.

In the manner of a poet, he first envisaged, then persistently willed and, in the face of all kinds of difficulties, effectively realized his plan for a House for the Relief of Suffering; he made it functional, using all the modern resources of science and technology. He decorated it tastefully, giving it a rich and dignified character; it cared for the poor free of charge and was not ungenerous towards the rich; the same care and treatment and loving attention was offered to all alike. So, on the dry rock of Gargano, among almond trees and sweetly scented Indian figs, rose up a hospital so modern that its opening was attended by the most renowned figures of the entire medical world.

This institution which caused Padre Pio such suffering and through which he was able to arouse great Christian generosity in so many hearts is the happiest and most authentic expression of evangelical charity.

It is strange, really marvellous, that such a humble friar from a poor region of southern Italy – as poor as it was then – who had grown up in the austere atmosphere of a Capuchin friary, should have had such a clear vision of a hospital such as this and should have wanted it so badly; it was the kind of hospital that another man from a quite different time and with different circumstances and educational background would never have dreamed of; nor had he seen it, would he have been able to appreciate and understand it.

For Padre Pio wanted the poor patient to be cared for and treated by qualified personnel; to this end, he wished to employ all the resources of science in a comfortable and dignified setting; he sought in this imaginative way to eliminate the depressing atmosphere of the traditional 'hospice' where the poor are humiliated because the staff serve them nothing but the crumbs which fall from the rich man's table – and, as the Gospel tells us, those crumbs are meant for dogs.

Padre Pio who had lovingly espoused poverty had understood the immense dignity of the poor in the Church;

in the light of the faith, sole guide of his thoughts and actions, he clearly saw the Lord Jesus present in the poor and, as he himself so finely expressed it, doubly present in the sick poor.

Padre Pio believed quite literally in the anticipated sentence of the Last Judgement: 'I was hungry and you gave me food, I was sick and you took care of me . . . Just as you did it to one of the least of these who are members of my family, you did it to me . . .'

And he wished every attention to be given to Jesus, the only Lord; had not Jesus complained to Simon the Pharisee that he, as host, had denied him the usual attentions given to an important guest? 'I entered your house; you gave me no water for my feet . . . you gave me no kiss . . . you did not anoint my head . . .' And the Lord had concluded that compared with the common prostitute, 'You loved less!' We cannot love Jesus less . . . When we open our doors to the sick we sense his presence and give him every attention . . . and even if he is hidden beneath a veil of misery, we adore him!

This is the new style of charity: new only insomuch as the Gospel has revealed in Jesus the name of the poor person, humble and defenceless, whose anonymous voice is already to be heard in the pages of the Old Testament. This is a new style of charity because even after the Good News has been preached to the poor for centuries, human egotism has all too often held the poor in contempt.

So, following Jesus' example, Padre Pio made himself poor and humble; by his fraternal identification with the poor, he sought to give them, on the spiritual plane, the succour that riches give to the wealthy on the material plane. He demonstrated to a secularized society the value of Christ's charity and poverty.

But Padre Pio's conformity to Christ is most evident in his suffering . . . his life was one of continual suffering and the similarity of his sufferings to those of Christ is only too obvious! First of all, there were incredulity and persecution on the part of those who could and should have been the first to understand, while it was the crowds of humble and sincere folk who flocked to the Church of Our Lady of Grace and to Padre Pio's confessional and — to borrow St Luke's words (Luke 6:18) — 'they had come to hear him and to be healed of their diseases; and all in the crowd were trying to touch him for power came out from him and healed all of them.'

Padre Pio experienced two periods of particularly intense suffering: the first was when his name had begun to be widely known because of the veneration in which he was held by the poor people of God and the extraordinary phenomena which drew such attention to the friar of Gargano were under discussion, while the austerity of his humble life and his zealous preaching and hidden ministry upset the local clergy and provoked a crisis in the Church in Manfredonia; there were accusations of monstrous infidelity, dishonest connivance and talk of 'raising up an abomination in the holy place.'

These wretched men, found their own ministry put to shame by Padre Pio's holy life and exemplary priesthood, but in the end people listened to their denunciations of the humble friar as an exhibitionist and hypocrite who was not only deluded but downright fraudulent with regard to the charismatic gifts which had won him the trust of the faithful masses.

When he was condemned by higher authority, who had reached their verdict without benefit of an objective inquiry, he submitted, as he always did to the decisions of his superiors, with prompt, silent obedience.

The evangelist's words drew attention to Jesus' silence amid the clamour of his accusers – a silence which greatly astonished the Roman judge; it was in such silence that Padre Pio spent forty years of inner torment.

He was talked about and written about; people condemned and derided him . . . and he was silent.

Silence. It is the very element of the ascetic life; it is the precondition for dialogue with God, for the interior life; it is from silence that springs each meaningful word which is to bring light and strength to humankind. It was in a mysterious silence that Moses, Elijah and John the Baptist prepared for their great missions . . . Jesus who is the living and eternal Word of the Father, the one Word of truth and life, lived in silence for thirty years . . . But silence becomes heroic when a man preserves it in the face of calumny, when he does not react to insults, does not stand up for his rights, does not accuse others of bullying, injustice, crime . . .

And so the mysterious drama moved into its second act. The truth had come out: the humble friar's life was manifestly authentic, yet his defeated enemies, seething with old grievances, launched another attack of calumny centred this time on his latest financial dealings; he became the target of a fresh persecution, conducted with incredible boldness and cynical cruelty. He was indeed the defenceless man of the Beatitudes: poor, meek, persecuted for the sake of justice.

Padre Pio was saddened by the fact that unauthorized persons were trying to control the income of the House for the Relief of Suffering — income which came from the charity of his spiritual children. He was certainly right to safeguard the intentions of the donors and in order to do so had been granted power to dispose of the money as if it were his, despite his vow of poverty and as long as his religious superiors did not relieve him of this duty, under the vow of obedience, he remained humbly and quietly firm in this matter . . .

But the thing that caused him the deepest anguish and made him agonize like Christ in the Garden of Olives was not that he suffered for the Church — in that case he would have taken comfort from the blessedness promised to those who suffer for the sake of the Gospel — but that he suffered from the Church. Now the Church is a community transformed by the Spirit of Christ into a wonderful sacrament of salvation and it was churchmen themselves who were polluting this community with their wretched greed, ambition, meanness and dishonesty . . . He knew the bitterness of arbitary procedures, harsh dealings, insults and scorn but he endured his cruel sufferings without complaint or retaliation . . . He was isolated from his friends and like Jesus he could say, 'I looked in vain for someone to comfort me' . . . Instead of friends he had enemies, wretched, mediocre types who could not bear the sight of a more virtuous man. His own brothers who had hitherto been his strength and stay, actually became his tormentors and those who, according to Capuchin tradition, should have been a support to him in his old age, miserably betrayed him with the sacrilegious kiss of the traitor.

Providence, too, was silent and, as in the Lord's passion, allowed men to give vent to their passions without thwarting their plans by divine intervention: 'My God, my God,' the old friar, sick and weary, must have groaned in the depths of his heart, 'why have you forsaken me?'

He never failed in humility, nor in obedience or charity . . . His faithfulness remained undiminished. And in spite of the constant suffering due to old age, fatigue, fasting, asthma and interior anguish, he continued to be a source of spiritual light, hope, generosity and love to the souls who turned to him for help.

Perhaps the greatest thing about Padre Pio — the poor friar of San Giovanni, known and loved the world over — is his long, silent, enduring, almost stubborn yet so humble, love for the Church, his fidelity to the Church, his complete availability which made him in the first place willing to prepare so calmly to leave for Spain and then, in all simplicity to renounce his fondest dream and his most cherished earthly accomplishment . . .

At a time when, as far as he knew, he faced the excruciating pain of exile from his native land, his only response was an affectionate letter full of loyalty and filial devotion to the Apostolic See . . . Then he returned to his habitual silence.

Padre Pio was poor: he had always been so, even when, by special privilege, he was allowed to register the House for the Relief of Suffering in his own name; in fact this was only a legal form to ensure that the House fulfilled its original aim.

But despite his extreme poverty he left a legacy, a precious inheritance: his example, his spirit, his prayer, his charity, his communion of faith and love with his order (of which Paul VI declared him a model member) and with God's holy Church . . .

It is our duty to benefit from that rich patrimony and to make it fruitful. All too often, it is out of purely natural individualism and not from true Christian motives that we seek the protection of saintly souls; but maybe it is God's loving purpose that they should be instead an example to us, a shining example, always to hand, which helps us towards that one true end for which we can usefully live and work: a greater conformity to Christ the Lord!

Chapter 25

How Paul VI missed visiting Padre Pio

In the early sixties, Padre Pio underwent real persecution even by the Vatican. And this happened despite the fact that the Pope, John XXIII, had a great love for the friar of Pietrelcina. It also took place during the Second Vatican Council which was to bring so many innovations to the Church, raising such hopes in the hearts of Catholics. The restrictions imposed on Padre Pio by the Holy Office (these even forbade him to receive and send letters and to see anyone but his relatives) gradually lessened from 1963 onwards but it was Paul VI, in January 1964, a few months after his election to the Supreme Pontificate (21 June 1963) who withdrew all restrictions on the peaceful pursuit of the friar's priestly ministry. Paul VI had a deep respect and devotion for Padre Pio and had shown it on several occasions. So no one was very surprised when the news leaked out in February 1967 that he was going to visit the stigmatic friar. I was one of the first to get wind of this, and the photographer Pietro D'Alessandro and I rushed to San Giovanni Rotondo where I wrote the following article for a weekly paper.

Towards ten o'clock on a cold February evening, a large black car drew up in front of the main entrance of the House for the Relief of Suffering at San Giovanni Rotondo. Because of the late hour and the rainy weather the streets of the Gargano village were deserted. An elderly uniformed chauffeur got out of the black Mercedes and walked cautiously towards the ground floor of the magnificent hospital built at Padre Pio's instigation with donations from the faithful all over the world. After an excited conversation with the doctor on duty and a sister, who seemed to be expecting the nocturnal visit, the unknown driver returned to the car, opened the back door and helped out a priest who went up the steps to the hospital where he stayed for two hours. He was the Apostolic Visitor, Monsignor Mino Maccari, who had come straight from the Holy See.

Towards midnight, the mysterious car turned into the road to Monte Sant'Angelo in the Gargano region. On the way, the driver swerved carelessly and the car went off the road into a ditch where it was stuck. After a worrying half-hour wait, a lorry came along and thanks to the help of the two drivers the car was put back on the road.

It was about two o'clock when the Mercedes stopped again, in front of the Shrine of San Michele Arcangelo which had from ancient times been a centre of pilgrimage attracting folk from all over Italy and also the rest of the world. Why should an Apostolic Visitor have made a nocturnal visit to the Shrine of San Michele? Several days were to pass before the truth emerged about this unexpected visit by Monsignor Maccari to San Giovanni Rotondo. The forthcoming event, for which this was the preparation, was indeed exceptional: Paul VI was coming to San Giovanni Rotondo to meet Padre Pio. The apostolic visitor had come to check on the route to be taken by the pope to San Giovanni and to forestall any possible problems connected with such an important and delicate visit.

Today, as we have already seen, Padre Pio enjoys the esteem of Paul VI who, while he was Archbishop of Milan and the battle against the friar of Pietrelcina was at its height, wrote to him these words, 'If you have to leave San Giovanni Rotondo, there's always my diocese, which is large enough to accommodate even you.' And now that Padre Pio's health was becoming worse all the time, the news that the Holy Father was coming to San Giovanni Rotondo took on a new complexion. Certainly the official announcement of Paul VI's proposed visit to San Giovanni was made with the utmost caution. The Church is known to be very prudent in such cases: an official announcement of the Pope's visit to Padre Pio would seem to endorse the view that the friar was a 'living saint' or at least it would lend official approval to the special quality of the stigmatic friar. So there were two possible interpretations of the visit: Paul VI was going to the Shrine of San Michele at Monte Sant'Angelo as several of his predecessors had done, and while visiting the House for the Relief of Suffering he would meet Padre Pio, or it was Padre Pio who was going to pay his respects to the Pope on the occasion of the Supreme Pontiff's visit to the Shrine of San Michele.

The second interpretation was not readily credible on account of Padre Pio's state of health. At that time he was weary and exhausted; it was extremely painful for him to stay on his feet even for a few minutes at a time. In order to take a single step he had to be supported by two of his brothers. A journey to Monte Sant'Angelo would have been a tremendous physical strain for him; he would only have been able to make the journey in an ambulance.

Padre Pio was told about the distinguished visitor: at first he was excited, then he said in subdued and plaintive tones, 'How am I going to get to Monte Sant'Angelo and prostrate myself before the pope and receive his blessing – how am I going to do it? How? I can't walk! O Lord, help me!'

'Father, maybe His Holiness will come here to you, to visit our hospital!'

'It's not possible. I'm not worthy, I'm not worthy . . . I can only pray for the Holy Father, that the Virgin will give him the strength to fulfil his mission of peace and he's in my prayers every day! But I'm not worthy, not worthy . . . I am just a poor soul . . .'

Paul VI's visit was to have followed this itinerary: Rome, taking the Autostrada del Sole as far as Avellino; a stop at Ariano Irpino to see the earthquake victims just over the border of the province of Puglia; then Foggia. From Foggia to Manfredonia, than along about thirty kilometres of smooth state highway to San Giovanni Rotondo. It would be seven hours' driving in all. Paul VI's visit to San Giovanni would have made a deep impression on the inhabitants of the area, simple folk, attached to their traditions; they looked on Padre Pio as the representative of their region.

On Palm Sunday they told the stigmatic friar of the Pope's proposed visit. He was praying in his cell; they gave him a small palm which he kissed slowly. His face look emaciated, he was moaning softly and his brown wool mittens were soaked with blood. He had had them changed at least four times in half a day. Since 1920, each year in Holy Week, Padre Pio da Pietrelcina 'relived' the passion. His

109

temperature would rise alarmingly, enough to break an ordinary thermometer. His eyes would glaze and he would moan piteously. Seated in an old armchair, he would recite several rosaries.

We had visited Padre Pio during the time just before Easter to have first-hand knowledge of his state of health. We went up to his cell. He was seated in the only armchair. The cell measures a few square metres; on the right as you went in, there was a small cabinet full of letters and donations; on the left was another cabinet also full of letters and boxes of medicine which he never used. A bed stood at the far end of the room on the left; on the wall was a large painting of Our Lady of Grace and a crucifix; there was a washbasin near the window. The friar who was with us announced our arrival:

'Father, here are some friends from Rome.'

'And what do thcy want with me?'

'To greet you and receive your blessing.'

We came forward at once and knelt before Padre Pio and shook hands with him.

'Ah! Don't squeeze!' His face was twisted with pain.

'Sorry, Father, we didn't mean to hurt you.'

'What do you want with me?' repeated Padre Pio.

'Just to greet you and to receive your blessing so that I can feel closer to God.'

'That's too easy! You should pray to the Lord yourself, not expect me to do it for you!'

'But my prayers are those of a sinner, they can't be heard by the Lord.'

'What are you saying? The Lord is near all those who pray sincerely and even those who don't pray at all, because God's mercy is infinite.'

'Father, you winced when I shook hands with you. Is it that you have more pain in the time just before Easter?'

'What are you here for? Out, out, throw him out!'

And he pointed to the door. The friar who was with us took us by the arm and as he went out with us he said:

'You've made him angry, you've made him angry . . .'

The next day I met him again in the passage on his way to church and he said to me:

'You again! What do you want now?'

110

'Father, I'd like to be forgiven for my impertinence yesterday.'

'And who am I to forgive?' Then, placing his hand on my head he said:

'Eh! the blessed young people!'

Heartened by this, I went on:

'Father, we journalists sometimes go too far, but our readers want to know so many things and we have to satisfy them . . .'

'By writing packs of lies . . . as you do.'

We remained in the passage watching the stigmatic friar as he walked away, supported by two of his brothers. We could hear the sound of his sandals as he shuffled along the old stone floor, coughing at frequent intervals; we saw him making his painful way up the staircase leading to the church, stopping on every step.

We saw him again later in the small new sitting-room next to his cell. It was ten o'clock; his doctor, Professor Sala, was with him and Padre Pio seemed very tired. We plucked up the courage to ask him:

'Father, how do you feel?'

'And of what interest is that to you? You're not my doctor, are you?'

Professor Sala smilingly came to my aid:

'Father, these journalists want to know everything — you have to understand them.'

Emboldened by Professor Sala's support, I rallied and asked:

'Father, did you know I was born in a house where a saint once lived?'

'And who was that saint?'

'Saint Gerard Majella, who is much venerated at Mater-domini in the province of Avellino. I was born in Lacedonia in the house where Gerard Majella lived for many years and worked miracles.'

'And what do you mean by that — that you feel safer?'

'No, Father, I mean that it's lovely to live where a saint lived, but it's even better to speak to a saint . . .'

'Go away, get out!'

This time he had a sudden outburst of temper and the rest of his words were lost in a fit of coughing. While Professor

Sala tried to calm him down, I walked quickly away. Later, Professor Sala, who was seeing Padre Pio every morning at nine, said to us:

'He is a very difficult patient but I am very happy to be looking after him.'

We met Professor Sala in his mayor's office at San Giovanni Rotondo. He is a warm and pleasant man, well-known and loved. We asked him:

'Professor, why on earth did you agree to become mayor of San Giovanni Rotondo?'

'It was Padre Pio who agreed to my name being added to the list of candidates for local government. Many of my friends had asked me to go into local government to try and get the communists out of the municipality, as they had been in power for many years. I've never been involved in politics. After much persuasion from my friends, I asked Padre Pio if I should accept the candidature. Padre Pio said to me, "Put yourself on the list and choose good men." So now here I am.'

Professor Sala was born at Merate in northern Italy and has lived with his family at San Giovanni Rotondo since Padre Pio worked a 'miracle' for his second son, Paolo. The following is Professor Sala's story:

'This is the first time I've told anyone why I came to San Giovanni Rotondo. In 1955 my son Paolo was seriously ill: I feared for his life. In my desperation I went to Padre Pio and asked for his prayers. And the good friar said to me, "Don't worry, your son will get well and will be the liveliest of all. But stay here in San Giovanni Rotondo: the hospital really needs doctors." After a few days, Paolo no longer showed any signs of his illness. As a doctor I could find no plausible scientific explanation and I believed it was a miracle. The difficult part was persuading my wife to move to the south. After some discussion, we made the decision. We've been here for eleven years now and my wife is very happy.

'We call Padre Pio "spiritual father" and I visit him every day. I always ask him the same questions: How is the cough? Do you feel well? Did you sleep last night? He always gives me the same answers, none of them true. So I know Padre Pio doesn't sleep, that if I prescribe medicine for him he

112

doesn't take it, and he regards every illness as a heaven-sent source of joy. Sometimes he has complained of a bad headache or rheumatic pains but I am sure he did this to please me, so that I could prescribe some remedy. Padre Pio suffers from bronchial catarrh. The acute arthritis he has had lately forces him to sit all the time; every step is a painful effort.'

We asked Professor Sala if the life Padre Pio led and the ills he suffered could be easily borne by an ordinary man. This was his answer:

'It's ridiculous that a man of eighty should be able to lead the kind of life that he does. It's an intense and exhausting life; I can't understand how his body endures all that pain. Padre Pio eats nothing, or hardly anything. At first, out of obedience to the rule, he used to sit at the friary table with his brothers taking a little hot soup and a piece of potato cake. Now, since he's been keeping to his cell, the tray with his frugal meal comes and goes untouched.'

Although Padre Pio was ill, humble pilgrims as well as scientists, politicians and industrialists continued to visit him to find comfort in a word from him; but it became more and more difficult because the friar had lost his former energy. Now he was spending much more time in prayer; his life was one of constant contact with the Lord.

During our visit, we had heard word of a crypt being built in which Padre Pio's mortal remains were to be laid to rest. As a result, we had difficulty getting into the crypt of the Church of Our Lady of Grace; there was talk of the crypt but no one had ever seen it. When we broached the subject with the friars, we met with an absolute refusal. So we thought up a little ruse. As any building work must be declared at the tax office, we went to the local administrator, Doctor Nunzio Conte, who showed us the relevant letter from the father guardian of the Capuchin friary who mentioned proposed building works without specifying their exact nature. On the pretext of making an official inspection, we went to the friary with the tax inspector, the camera well hidden and a sheaf of tax forms under our arms. The unsuspecting young friar who took us to the crypt had not the least idea that we were journalists.

One day Padre Pio had turned to one of his brothers and

said smilingly,'But look where they want to put me! They've already prepared my tomb.' Perhaps the good Capuchin friar would have liked to be buried near his beloved parents in the little cemetery of San Giovanni Rotondo. But it was thought fitting to find a dwelling for Padre Pio in the church where he had celebrated his 'interminable, mystical' holy Masses. He would not have dreamt of asking to be buried elsewhere; the Franciscan rule which had guided him throughout his life forbade him to ask.

After Pope Pius XII's words of praise in which he congratulated Padre Pio on a 'work inspired by the purest sense of evangelical charity', he now enjoyed the esteem of Pope Paul VI. The visit of the pope to San Giovanni Rotondo would have been the crowning event of the stigmatic friar's humble life of prayer and Christian charity. But Padre Pio was very troubled as soon as he heard the news. How could the pope meet him, a poor friar? What could he say to the Holy Father? All he could do was kneel and kiss his hand.

'I am not worthy,' exclaimed the friar of San Giovanni.

Chapter 26

The meeting with Aldo Moro

I often went to visit Padre Pio on my own but I also went many times with some friend of mine and above all with friends of the friar. Out of all these friends, I have nostalgic memories of one in particular, Monsignor Renato Luisi, Bishop of Bovino in the province of Foggia: a man of great culture and humanity, full of enterprise and always available to visitors.

Don Renato, as he was known throughout the diocese, had been a teacher of religious knowledge at Vincenzo Lanza School. I went several times to San Giovanni Rotondo with Don Renato to see Padre Pio. I remember that one time, in 1963, when we were with Padre Pio, I told them about some schoolboy pranks which had been viewed with great tolerance during the religious knowledge class. Padre Pio said, 'And what about the time when Don Renato threw you out, heretic that you are!' I turned to Don Renato in dismay as I recalled the episode which had got me thrown out of the classroom. This is how it happened: in the religious knowledge class Don Renato was explaining the value of Jesus' mission, his love for humanity and for his neighbour and the final sacrifice of the crucifixion for the redemption of the world. I asked him a rather impertinent question, 'But if Jesus who was omnipotent sacrificed himself even to death for humanity, does that mean that even he has need for humanity?' I should not have said it! I saw Don Renato raise his hand and point to the door, shouting 'Get out!' With bowed head, I left the room, astonished by such a negative reaction.

Turning to Padre Pio, I admitted to the episode; I smiled at Don Renato and said, 'With Padre Pio, I don't think I'd have been thrown out.' The friar said, 'Well, this time I'll throw you out because you're making me waste precious time.'

When I think of Don Renato, who died recently in Foggia, I also remember his great friendship with Aldo Moro;* he was in constant contact with Aldo and kept up a flourishing correspondence with him. They got to know each other at the meetings of the FUCI, the Federation of Young Catholic Students where Don Renato assumed the role not only of spiritual director but also of friend confidant to so many young men who were going into politics or public life. I remember that whenever Don Renato came to Rome, especially while Moro was prime minister, I went with him in my capacity as municipal councillor of Foggia, where I had been elected to local government in 1966 and as an alderman from 1971 onwards. We were always received by Moro's ever-faithful secretary, Tommaso Leucadito, who would tell us the local news in his pleasant Bari accent.

These meetings were always marked by the most warm and sincere friendship and Don Renato was obviously proud to have among his 'boys' a man of such stature as Moro who had risen to the top in politics. Even Aldo Moro, ever courteous, lost some of his proverbial reserve when he recalled the days of his youth. Aldo Moro also met Padre Pio. It was on 15 March 1968 and I was there along with some of the friar's most faithful fellow-workers. Padre Pio was known to have little sympathy with politicians and would become rather severe when he met them. But he had a deep respect for Aldo Moro, not only on account of the esteem in which he was held but also because of his profound humanity and spirituality. I believe that Moro lived in an environment in some ways alien to him. Although he was a realistic and thoroughly professional politician, he persisted in dreaming of a peaceful and just world unburdened by existential problems, free of organized malice and mindless violence. Sadly, he paid the highest and most terrible price for his high principles.** But his doctrine and personal rectitude will leave their mark on our age for years to come and will have a permanent place in the annals of democracy.

*Aldo Moro, the eminent statesman from the southern Italian town of Bari, was leader of the Christian Democratic Party and, more than once, prime minister of Italy.

**Aldo Moro was kidnapped and assassinated by terrorists, belonging to the Red Brigades.

To return to the meeting with Padre Pio, he was very welcoming. He asked things like, 'How often do you pray to the Lord during the day?' Then the two men went aside for a few minutes and, naturally, no one knows the subject of their private conversation.

Someone told how Padre Pio made a prophecy to Moro which was tragically fulfilled. All I remember, very clearly, is Padre Pio's expression as he turned to watch Moro walking away; he looked both affectionate and sad, as when one says farewell to a dear old friend, perhaps for the last time.

Chapter 27

Padre Pio's last years

I followed all the events of Padre Pio' s life with keen attention especially during his last years, when I was concerned with
his poor health. I quote here some articles I wrote during
that time and which seem of particular significance. The first
dates back to 30 May 1964.

These are anxious moments at San Giovanni Rotondo on
account of Padre Pio's health. The 'saint of Gargano' is
once again lying on a sickbed in his cell, forcing himself to
smile so as not to alarm the brothers looking after him. He
lies under a heavy woollen blanket, his face streaming with
perspiration: from time to time he groans but soon stifles
the sound as he is determined to suffer in silence.

'Padre Pio,' a friar said to him, 'you're suffering so much,
would you like to be moved to the House for the Relief of
Suffering where you would get more help?' Padre Pio could
speak only with great difficulty, but he answered, 'Suffering? But I'm not suffering, I'm begging Our Lady to give
me strength to go on praying with great fervour for suffering humanity. It's humanity that's suffering!'

It all happened unexpectedly last Wednesday afternoon.
Having retired as usual to his cell after lunch, he did not
come out for the evening ceremonies. At first the friars
thought he was just late; than as time went by and Padre
Pio still failed to appear at his cell door, they plucked up
courage and knocked discreetly. There was no response from
within. When the friars decided to go in, they found Padre
Pio writhing, face down on the bed, moaning feebly. The
poor friars were dazed for a few moments then rushed to
his assistance, lifting him up by his arms and placing him
on his back. When he saw them Padre Pio brightened visibly
and smiled at them.

'Padre Pio, whatever happpened to you? Do you feel ill?

My God, say something, don't keep us in suspense!' Padre Pio answered, 'Calm down, don't worry, it's nothing; I had some pain in my stomach or maybe somewhere else and I didn't have the strength to walk.' While he was saying this, a friar was running to fetch a doctor from the House for the Relief of Suffering.

Later Padre Pio smiled cheerfully at the doctor too, saying that every illness had its proper limits and it would all be over by the morning. But the trouble did not go away during the night. The sick man could not settle down in bed, he tossed and turned, trying to relieve the pain by finding a comfortable position. It was only towards four o'clock that the pain wore off and he was able to sleep. Meanwhile cars and coaches were starting to fill the square in front of the Friary of Our Lady of Grace, coming from all over Italy for the feast of Corpus Christi. Thousands of people were anxiously waiting for Padre Pio's Mass. But the minutes went by and the friar was not to be seen. At five o'clock a Capuchin friar took Padre Pio's place at the altar. The faithful were disappointed and also apprehensive. What had happened? But nothing was known officially, no one was saying anything. Only later, when many of the faithful went to stand beneath Padre Pio's window and saw figures going busily to and fro, silhouetted against the lighted room, did the news pass from mouth to mouth, naturally becoming twisted, exaggerated and distorted in the process.

Padre Pio was ill in bed. In the pouring rain, everyone prayed silently for his recovery. The hours went by and more cars arrived at San Giovanni Rotondo. For Padre Pio's devotees, Corpus Christi is the greatest feast their 'living saint' could celebrate. It is the feast of the Body of the Lord so dear to Padre Pio who contemplates the consecrated host in ecstasy every morning at the elevation, his eyes shining with a strange mystical light. The faithful say that Corpus Christi is Padre Pio's feast! On this day, the Mass is longer, much longer. Padre Pio stands gazing fixedly at the host as the minutes tick by: his heavy body weighs on the stigmata in his feet causing frightful pain which he either does not feel or accepts with joy. But this year he was unable to repeat his penitential prayer. He was forced to suffer on his humble bed.

On the afternoon of Corpus Christi itself while a vast crowd was waiting to see Padre Pio, at least for the evening ceremonies, we were near to his cell instead, and had escorted him to bed where he lay writhing in agony. We saw his face contorted with pain, his eyes half closed; on the bedside table was a bottle of water, a glass, a thermometer and a few medicines. We stayed just outside his cell door. We could hear clearly what was being said. The words we reported at the beginning were said slowly and with difficulty in a feeble voice. We saw a young friar come out of the cell in tears. 'No, Padre Pio, you musn't leave us, we need you and your prayers so badly!' he sobbed.

We were lucky enough to see Padre Pio at close quarters by means of a little ruse. We had been told of his illness on Wednesday night when we reached San Giovanni Rotondo after a long nerve-racking wait at the friary door, we took advantage of the bad weather (everyone was too busy hurrying indoors to notice us): we fell in with a doctor who was entering quickly and the friary porter evidently mistook us for infirmarians. This is how we were able to be the first to notify our readers of Padre Pio's alarming condition.

However, we were told very little about the nature of his illness. Understandably, everyone shut up like clams! But Padre Pio must have had stomach trouble; we saw him clutching his abdomen several times as if to ease the pain. The doctors did not seem unduly worried, maybe because the patient showed no signs of fever. All the same one has to bear in mind that Padre Pio is seventy-six and his constitution has been undermined not only by old age but also by constant deprivation.

On that occasion the doctors were right not to be so concerned. In fact Padre Pio recovered. But his health was already poor and he went on having alarming attacks at intervals. This is what I wrote when he was ill once in April 1965:

This is a very worrying time at San Giovanni Rotondo. Only vague and confused reports of Padre Pio's illness are filtering through to the outside world but all the news is alarming. It has been announced that Professor Cassano, director of the

School of Pathological Medicine at Rome University who is at present in the United States as personal physician to Aldo Moro, will shortly be arriving here: he was reached by a personal telephone call from San Giovanni Rotondo and has promised to be at the sick friar's bedside by Sunday morning without fail.

The village is full of the faithful from all over Italy: everyone is praying, many are in tears, there are sad faces on every side.

Unfortunately, as our own investigations confirmed, such alarm was justified. We went into the friary, we went up to the sick friar's cell, we spoke to the friars who are looking after him and met the attendant physicians; above all, we heard this most distressing news: for the first time, Padre Pio is in a very disturbed psychological state. But let us tell our story in due order. Yesterday afternoon, Professor Putoni arrived from Naples. The Professor − contrary to initial reports − did not hide his anxiety: in the course of a lengthy and thorough examination, he found Padre Pio very depressed, both mentally and physically; he found circulatory problems resulting from the thrombo-phlebitis from which he suffers; high temperature and frequent hot flushes in the face; he said it was a pity the friar had been given so many sedatives and ordered complete rest for a few days.

Padre Pio's health had began to give cause for alarm when, having celebrated Mass one day, he had asked his brothers to take him to his cell immediately. He stayed in bed that day and the next day managed to say Mass with great difficulty. The friars begged him not to tire himself but to no avail; Padre Pio answered in tones of sorrowful but fraternal rebuke, 'You're worrying about my health but not for the whole world which is ailing! Who, who is praying to the Lord?'

But even his strong will-power could not withstand the physical strain of that day. At the age of sixty-eight, infirm as he was, above all with the continual loss of blood through the stigmata, he could not afford to waste what strength he had left. And when one of the friars went to his cell the next morning to see how he was, Padre Pio smiled gently and said, 'This morning Jesus Christ will come to me! Patience! I don't feel I can go to his altar . . . The young friar was

121

disconcerted by this remark and could not but notify the superior of the community who came rushing to the narrow cell and administered communion to the sick friar shortly afterwards. After receiving the sacament, Padre Pio prayed and wept softly for a long time.

Naturally, Padre Pio has not celebrated Mass or heard confessions today either: he has been forbidden by the doctors to receive any visitors or to tire himself in any way, especially emotionally. The faithful have waited anxiously for several days now for Padre Pio's usual morning appearance at the high altar where he comes to say Mass; in vain have they waited for the amazing mystical spectacle of a rite lasting for two hours, the celebrant overcome with ecstasy.

Once more the friary is keeping an extremely low profile but such reserve encourages rather than curbs extravagant rumours; it makes people suspect the worst and feeds exaggerated fears and anxieties. There are so many rumours flying round that we cannot keep track of them all. And often they are contradictory. Yesterday, for example, an unnamed source, evidently seeking to promote optimism, had put it about that Padre Pio had said, 'Don't worry about me, I'll go on to ninety!' Today another anonymous source spread a rumour to the contrary. Padre Pio is reported to have said: 'It's time the Lord called me; I can no longer help my brothers.'

Unfortunately, of the two, the last is nearer the truth. We cannot confirm that Padre Pio said exactly those words but, as we have alredy mentioned, we managed to get into the friary and we came out convinced that that disconsolate remark corresponds to his present state of mind.

Having got into the friary, we managed to go as far as the dormitory passage where no outsiders are ever permitted to enter. We very cautiously edged as close as we could to the entrance of Padre Pio's cell, hoping to catch a glimpse of him or to pick up some news or first-hand impressions. Suddenly we saw a friar, one of those particularly devoted to him, coming out of his cell weeping. We went towards him and he told us through his sobs, 'Poor Padre Pio, he's never suffered like this before! I tried to comfort him by saying everyone is praying for his complete recovery and he asked me to pray for his death because he's tired of living by now . . .'

What struck the young friar most forcibly was the discouragement which, from the very start of this illness, had reduced Padre Pio to a state of mental depression such as he had never shown until then. The friars were used to seeing their brother always smiling, sometimes even joking, even when he was bedridden, as he often was. This time, however, he was disconsolate. This morning he said, 'Pray, pray for humanity which does not know what it is doing or where it is going . . . I look around me and see so much suffering! O Lord, enlighten the hearts of the peoples and lead them to peace and faith . . .'

What we have reported so far, saddens us. Now it remains to speak of things which astonish us. All those who have followed the campaign waged by this newspaper know of the unedifying events, the intrigues, the conflict of interests and the rancour surrounding Padre Pio's case. Well, in these very painful circumstances, there has been a resurgence of the same rancour and a renewed clash of interests.

In the past few days we have already mentioned a detail which puzzled many people: in spite of the fact that, thanks to Padre Pio, San Giovanni Rotondo boasts one of the most modern, efficient and well-equipped hospitals in the south of Italy, the doctors of the House for the Relief of Suffering have not always been allowed to attend the sick man as they had always done previously. The only doctor called to his bedside was one who had left the big hospital and only later was Professor Puntoni summoned from Naples. Yet the House for the Relief of Suffering has seven chief physicians and thirty-four doctors all of whom are noted for their experience as well as being devoted to the stigmatic friar, an extremely unusual patient.

Professor Franco Lotti, chief physician at the House for the Relief of Suffering, having asked in vain for permission to visit the invalid, succeeded in getting into the friary and up to Padre Pio's cell. The guardian of the friary, Father Carmelo, tried to stop him coming in but, during the lively discussion which ensued, Padre Pio recognized the voice of his old friend (Professor Lotti was the first to respond to Padre Pio's appeal and had transferred to San Giovanni Rotondo

123

from being assistant to Professor Savioli of Bologna) and called to him in a weak voice and asked the professor to come closer to him; he embraced him very warmly and sobbed as he said goodbye.

It is certainly difficult to understand why Professor Lotti and other doctors from Padre Pio's hospital were not allowed to attend the invalid. But that is what happened.

Professor Cassano, however, was summoned after this episode. When Professor Lotti returned from the friary he called all his colleagues together and it was they who decided to telephone to the United States to ask the famous professor to come. Professor Cassano who, with Professor Valdoni, is one of the consultants at the House for the Relief of Suffering, promised, as we said, that he would definitely be in San Giovanni Rotondo on Sunday morning. Personal physician to the Italian Prime Minister, who had asked him to accompany him on his official visit to the United States, Professor Cassano is a pathologist of international repute.

Needless to say, his arrival is awaited with great anxiety.

But Padre Pio recovered on that occasion, too. His health remained poor, he frequently suffered discomfort, but thanks partly to the summer weather, he had a certain period of physical well-being. During the summer at least he was able to follow his usual daily routine.

Chapter 28

The last Easter

Only three weeks after his meeting with Aldo Moro, Padre Pio was at death's door. Hearing the news, I rushed as usual to San Giovanni Rotondo, feeling sad and worried as I always did when I had to report of the friar's illnesses. This time the article I wrote was for the weekly magazine *Gente*:

Padre Pio da Pietrelcina has been hovering between life and death for three days. He started feeling ill on 17 April, Palm Sunday, and he recovered only on Wednesday 10 May. He spent nearly all the next day, Maundy Thursday, sitting on the bed in his cell saying the rosary. 'Bed' is really too good a word for a miserable camp cot. Although every year during Holy Week the stigmatic friar suffers more than usual and the blood flows more freely from his hands and feet, during the last few days the attendant physicians have been seriously worried. Padre Pio seems to be literally prostrate, his eyes have lost their former piercing quality and his extremely robust constitution seems to be on the verge of final collapse. The friar has been suffering from bronchitis but this time it is not just his respiratory tract that is affected: it is something more serious and less explicable medically; if we were not afraid of being misunderstood, we would say it was a mysterious illness.

We have known Padre Pio for years but never has his suffering seemed more terrible than in these past few days. He has already reached the venerable age of nearly eighty-one (on 25 May next) and each time the weather changes his asthma and bronchitis give him trouble; he can scarcely walk for his wounded feet; in order to leave his cell to hear confessions or celebrate Mass, he has to have two brothers to support him. This last Easter brought him not only joy but also suffering such as few others would be able to bear with such fortitude. Between Palm Sunday and the following

Wednesday, there has been a whole succession of doctors in the little cell where the 'saint of Gargano' lay quietly gazing at the picture of Our Lady of Grace opposite the bed. Padre Pio said not a word during his recent illness; when the doctors inquired kindly after his symptoms, he responded with a faint smile or by closing his eyes. More than once he cried out, 'Leave me in peace to pray to the Lord! It's nearly Easter and humanity needs so many prayers.'

For these three long days as usual he touched no food; only once during the night he murmured, 'I'm thirsty.' The brother who was with him hastily passed him a glass of water but Padre Pio, looking at him in a fatherly way, exclaimed, 'What? Our Lord was very thirsty on the cross, too, and they gave him a sponge dipped in vinegar. Why should I drink water?' This is how Padre Pio prepared for Easter: stretched out on his old cot of a bed, tormented by an illness which medical science had failed to diagnose, suffering from very high fever and raging thirst, his body racked with shooting pains and his soul absorbed in prayer.

It had always been like this, even in previous years. During the days of the Lord's passion, the friar would fall into a deep spiritual and physical prostration: his stigmata would open even further, the blood would soon soak the woollen mittens he always wore on his hands, his feet would swell alarmingly. Each year, however, he would be happy to offer up his sufferings to the Lord at a time when all Christendom was re-living the sacrifice of Christ. But this year his sudden mysterious illness had completely exhausted him.

We were with Padre Pio on Good Friday, the day on which his suffering usually passed the limits of human endurance. All through the previous night he had prayed in his cell, sitting on his cot. Dozens of times the brother with him had changed his mittens and wiped clean his rosary which was covered with blood and sweat. We saw a different Padre Pio. He looked so exhausted, with his lean, emaciated face, his white hair and beard. It was the first time we had been able to sustain his gaze: we looked at him for a long time and for the first time his piercing eyes did not force us to lower ours. We have been visiting Padre Pio for years and for years we have never been able to endure the way he looked at us with those searching, sometimes accusing

126

eyes of his. Now he was before us, his eyes still bright, but with something missing. We could look into his eyes and see wonder and a great gentleness there. We knelt before him and kissed his hand without touching it for fear of hurting him.

'Hey! Have you got out of the habit of shaking hands?' said Padre Pio in a faint voice.

'Just this once I'm not shaking hands with you because I know you suffer terribly on Good Friday.'

'And what do you know? You always think you know everything and you don't know anything,' answered Padre Pio almost dryly; and for a moment he seemed like his old self, brusque at times when people passed personal remarks or made him out to be almost superhuman.

'Father, how are you feeling? I heard you haven't been well,' I asked him, taking courage once more.

'Well, my son, how could I be healthy at my age?'

'Father, I wish you another thousand years: the world needs your prayers. Don't you see how many people come to you to get a word of comfort?'

'I would very much like to pray to the Lord for the good of humanity but it's not up to me. Look, with your questions you're making me waste my time and not letting me pray to the Lord!'

'Did you hear they're negotiating peace with Vietnam? Are you pleased?'

'You ask me if I'm pleased about peace in the world, I who am suffering for the sake of peace? I always pray to the Lord that he will enlighten the leaders of the nations and give them the strength to resolve conflicts with brotherly love', answered Padre Pio looking up to heaven.

'Father, would you say a few words to our readers?'

'Tell them to pray for the peace of the world, to visit the sick, the suffering and those in prison. Tell them to be good in the name of the Lord and may they know how to use the great gift of life, living in the grace of God with prayer and good works.'

At that point a friar politely asked us to leave so as not to tire Padre Pio. As we crossed the small passage in the friary we noticed, in the cell next to Padre Pio's, a brand new wheelchair: it was the chair which was given to him three months ago and which the brothers of the small Friary of Our Lady of Grace had hoped would be of great help to the stigmatic friar in his daily round in the friary. But Padre Pio never wanted to get into it. The only time he was forced to do so, he cried out, weeping bitterly, 'No, I don't want to be off the ground; in the chair it seems as if I'll never be able to touch the ground!' They let him have his way and now, if he wants to move, he has to be carried.

Even during the Holy Saturday ceremonies when a huge crowd had been awaiting Padre Pio in the old friary church since the early hours of the afternoon, he did not want to use the wheelchair, as his thoughtful brothers had very gently suggested, to spare him excessive fatigue as the service was to be fairly lengthy.

It was on Holy Saturday that we went back to see him. He was alone on the spacious verandah which gives onto the friary garden, sitting in a wicker armchair. He was holding a white handkerchief with which he constantly mopped his brow as the temperature was quite high. While the photographer Antonio Lo Muzio took a few photographs, we knelt down and asked his blessing. Padre Pio said:

'How many times do you want to get blessed, my son? You were here yesterday and today; what are you up to?'

We were not at all surprised at this, knowing how brusque he could be and how good-hearted, too, so we replied:

'We are always pleased to see you, Father, and to receive your blessing.'

'And to take photos of me and write nonsense about me . . .'

'I don't write nonsense, Father; I say what I've seen for myself and the things that other reliable witnesses say about you.'

'Then it must be those other witnesses who talk nonsense,' pursued Padre Pio, looking us in the eye.

'Father, some time ago there was talk of Paul VI coming to San Giovanni Rotondo: a trip that was postponed because of the Pope's sudden illness. If the visit were still to take place, what would you say to him?'

'It would be too wonderful and I don't deserve such a thing. I am a poor friar who prays to the Lord and I only want the Pope to say a prayer for me too. If I had the strength, I'd go to Rome to kneel at his feet. I can just pray that the Lord will give the Pope many graces!'

While he was looking through the verandah windows, three friars came in and asked Padre Pio to go to the church with them as the Easter ceremonies were due to start. Padre Pio was helped out of his wicker chair; each step was agony for him, his feet were incredibly swollen, his breathing laboured. Although the pain made him wince he found the strength to say the rosary. The church was packed with people from all over the world; a great number of men had made their confessions in the hope of receiving communion from Padre Pio. The 'saint of San Giovanni' has not administered communion for ten years now; he just hears confessions. It seems that this year he had decided to administer communion. In fact a great crowd was gathered in front of the altar; Padre Pio remained seated and taking the ciborium in his hands, gave the consecrated host to the people, who were deeply moved. The friars present were astonished; how could Padre Pio be giving communion like this after ten years? Was this really Padre Pio's most beautiful Easter? The communion lasted for more than an hour, so many were the faithful who wished to receive the consecrated host from Padre Pio's own hands. And Padre Pio gave no sign of tiredness, his face showed nothing but joy as he looked at the joyful and hopeful folk assembled there.

During the celebration of the Mass we took careful note of all Padre Pio's movements. At the elevation we saw his face light up, he was gazing at the host which had only been raised up for a few minutes. Suddenly Padre Pio's arms fell back onto the altar; and to think that for some time back the elevation had lasted as much as twenty minutes, sometimes more: it seemed as if Padre Pio was speaking to the host, so intent was his gaze as he contemplated it, his face as if transfigured. But today his mystical ecstasy lasted only a few minutes.

Padre Pio is tired, his limbs can no longer bear the weight of the years and the sufferings which afflict him. At a certain point, tears began to flow from Padre Pio's eyes; he wept quietly until the end of the ceremony.

Chapter 29

The death of Padre Pio

On 20 September 1968 Padre Pio celebrated the fiftieth anniversary of the receiving of the stigmata. Having said Mass, he appeared at his cell window and blessed the faithful although he was ill. He was unable to raise his hand.

On 22 September he received prayer groups and blessed them with deep emotion. At six o'clock he appeared for the last time at his cell window to bless the faithful gathered there in prayer. He smiled but his face looked weary and emaciated; every step brought on his asthma and his breathing would become laboured. Turning to the brothers who were supporting him he exclaimed, 'Soon I'll be sparing you the trouble of taking me to Mass!' A dramatic prophecy indeed; that same evening at nine o'clock Padre Pio's life began to draw to its close.

9 p.m. Padre Pio has been in his cell for only a few hours, that is, since he gave his last blessing to his spiritual children after the evening Mass from the gallery of the church next to the friary. Father Pellegrino, one of the friars looking after him, takes over at nine o'clock, going into the cell next to Padre Pio.

9.15 p.m. Padre Pio calls Father Pellegrino on the intercom. He asks him what time it is. He recites a Hail Mary and asks to be left alone.

10 p.m. Father Pellegrino is called once more on the intercom by Padre Pio. His voice sounds heavy and his speech is laboured. He rushes into the next-door cell and finds the stigmatic friar with the rosary in his hands and his eyes staring. Again he asks what time it is and asks him to stay with him and say a few prayers.

11 p.m. Father Pellegrino looks in on Padre Pio and wishes him a good night and goes back to his cell having turned out the passage light. He starts to feel a bit anxious. He stays awake.

Midnight. The intercom rings in Father Pellegrino's cell. It is Padre Pio again. He rushes into the friar's cell again. Padre Pio's face is very pale, his breathing laboured. Padre Pio whispers, 'Stay here!' and after a few moments, 'What time is it?'

'It's twelve minutes past midnight,' answers Father Pellegrino.

'Hey, lad, have you said Mass?'

'Padre Pio, it's a bit early to say Mass!'

'Well, this morning you can say it for me,' Padre Pio went on, with a slight smile.

'Ah yes, you know I say Mass every morning for your intentions!'

23 September 1968 12.20 a.m.: Padre Pio turns to Father Pellegrino and asks him to hear his confession. Immediately afterwards in a slow and weary voice he says, 'Listen! If the Lord calls me today, ask my brothers and all my spiritual children to forgive me for all the troubles I've caused them and ask them all to pray for my soul.'

At these heart-breaking words, Father Pellegrino came even closer to Padre Pio, and knelt down beside him.

'Padre Pio, I think the Lord will let you live for a long time yet but, if you are right, may I ask your blessing for the brothers, all your spiritual children and for your hospital patients?'

'Yes, yes,' answered Padre Pio, 'I bless them all. Or rather I beg the superior to give them my blessing, on my behalf.'

12.50 a.m. Padre Pio, who had shown signs of being uncomfortable in bed, turns on his side and asks to get up. 'It's better for me to get up: I can't rest here in bed.' And he is helped to sit in the nearby armchair.

12.55 a.m. 'Well, let's go back to the room,' says Padre Pio almost in a whisper. Father Pellegrino goes to help him out of the chair but is unable to do so. Padre Pio has become very heavy, like a tree trunk. His arms dangle helplessly by his side. It is impossible to support his weight.

1 a.m. Padre Pio's face turns very pale; his brow beads with sweat, his breathing becomes laboured. Father Pellegrino wipes away the sweat. He thinks it is an asthma attack such as Padre Pio has often had. And he is not mistaken because Padre Pio himself, feeling the need for air, says to him, 'Take my chair outside!'

1.10 a.m. Padre Pio, still in his chair, is pushed back into his cell by Father Pellegrino. His lips have gone livid, his eyes seem to be full of tears, his brow is streaming with sweat. Father Pellegrino, convinced by now of his confrère's critical condition, moves to call other people. Padre Pio realizes what he is about, and says, 'Hey, lad, don't wake anyone!'

1.15 a.m. There are two friars with Padre Pio: Father Guglielmo and Father Pellegrino. The last runs to telephone Professor Sala, mayor of San Giovanni Rotondo and the friar's doctor, to ask him to come quickly to the friary.

1.25 a.m. Padre Pio sits in the wicker chair and says the last rosary of his earthly life. He speaks the words syllable by syllable, there are long pauses, he no longer touches the beads, his fingers are closed; the only words he can be heard saying, with difficulty, are '*Ave Maria . . .*'

1.30 a.m. Professor Sala arrives and thinks it is the usual asthma attack; he prepares an injection.

1.35 a.m. Having given the injection, Professor Sala notices that the breathing is no easier and decides to put Padre Pio back in the armchair. But even then the friar shows no sign of improvement. His breathing is slow and difficult. He repeats over and over, 'Jesus, Mary, Jesus, Mary!'

1.41 a.m. The whole friary is up. The news of Padre Pio's serious condition travels from cell to cell.

1.45 a.m. A small cup of coffeee is taken to the cell; Father Guglielmo tries to give Padre Pio a spoonful but the coffee trickles off the friar's lips.

1.50 a.m. Padre Pio's mind is fully alert; he watches everything going on around him, he goes on saying the rosary; his lips move.

2.05 a.m. Padre Pio's agony begins; his heartbeats slow down considerably.

2.09 a.m. Father Paolo administers the holy oil to the stigmatic friar; Padre Pio's lips move as he says, 'Jesus, Mary . . .'

2.12 a.m. The doctors start cardiac massage in a dramatic bid to keep the 'saint of San Giovanni' from death.

2.15 a.m. The cardiac massage continues; Padre Pio's eyes open for a moment; it will be the last time.

2.21 a.m. Everyone stands around Padre Pio; they all look at him, their eyes filled with tears; he seems to be asleep; his face shows no sign of pain or suffering.

2.25 a.m. Professor Sala takes Padre Pio's pulse; it is extremely weak.

2.26 a.m. Padre Pio's head leans slightly towards his right shoulder; his breathing can still be heard.

2.27 a.m. Padre Pio's rosary falls to the floor; Father Guglielmo picks it up.

2.28 a.m. The friar's breathing is barely audible.

2.29 a.m. The cell is full of people. There is a profound silence.

2.30 a.m. A deep sigh, the death rattle, and Padre Pio's head falls onto his right shoulder. Padre Pio is dead. So dies a 'saint'.

Chapter 30

The funeral

As soon as Padre Pio had bowed his head and breathed his last a mournful toll of bells sounded from the Friary of Our Lady of Grace. In the silence of the night all the inhabitants of San Giovanni Rotondo were alerted by the sound of the sad news conveyed by the bells. From window after window rose exclamations of astonishment as the word went round, 'Padre Pio is dead.' 'Our saint is no more.'

In a few minutes the lights were on all over the village; the first faithful came rushing from their houses to the friary. At four o'clock the square in front of the friary was full of people praying and begging to see the stigmatic friar for the last time.

Meanwhile, in the small cell number 5, Padre Pio had been clothed in a new brown habit, a cross laid on his breast, his rosary in his hands; he looked as if he were asleep.

The telephone rang incessantly in San Giovanni Rotondo with calls from all parts of Italy and all over the world. Everyone wanted to know, everyone was distressed. The police started to arrive from Foggia; it was becoming necessary to control the huge crowds which were beginning to converge on the friary.

It was decided to place Padre Pio on a glass-covered bier in the Church of Our Lady of Grace so that he could be seen by all.

I, too, wanted to see him for the last time; after queueing for three hours, I managed to kiss the glass case of his bier. It was estimated that one hundred thousand people came to San Giovanni Rotondo for the friar's funeral. Most of them were his closest spiritual children, his relatives, the faithful who had met him so often and many who had never seen him close enough. There were indescribable scenes of emotion, grief and tears shed for the 'saint' of Gargano.

The funeral lasted two hours; flowers rained down on the

coffin as it passed by. The bearers paused at every step as hands stretched out to touch the coffin and kisses were continually blown towards it. Every few feet of the way was marked by some speech or commemoration: the mayor, Professor Sala, the scientist Enrico Medi, the superior of the friary, Father Carmelo, the superior general, Father Clementino da Punta Ala, and many others. Each bore witness to the friar's works, each spoke sadly of his passing.

The coffin also passed beneath the windows of the House for the Relief of Suffering for a last goodbye to his hospital patients; forgetting their infirmities, they were all looking out of the windows and crowded the balconies, some of them supported by nurses, to greet their benefactor for the last time.

The shadows were already falling over San Giovanni Rotondo when Padre Pio's coffin returned to the Church of Our Lady of Grace to be buried in the crypt beneath.

He rests there now, among his own people, near his sick folk, in a black marble tomb where dozens of people come day after day to pour out their faith-filled prayers to the stigmatic friar.

'Pray, pray and do good.' These words, so often repeated by Padre Pio, still spur us on today in our life as committed Christians, two decades after his death.

Chapter 31

Father Lino da Prato remembers Padre Pio

It was Father Lino da Prato who told me on 19 September 1968 that Padre Pio was ill in bed while the photograhper D'Alessandro and I were convinced that we had met him in the friary minutes earlier. Father Lino was the superior of the Sant'Anna friary at Foggia and was a good friend of mine; he often went with me to visit Padre Pio, acting as my protector, often helping me to carry out interviews and journalistic work.

When I was about to write this book of tribute to the memory of the stigmatic friar, I went to see Father Lino and told him I wanted to make an appointment to discuss with him the most significant stages of Padre Pio's life. Instead of a conversation or interview Father Lino let me have the following 'memoir' which I have made mine by a few slight alterations.

My last meeting with dear Padre Pio 'that most human figure of a friar consumed with love for his fellows', took place on the terrace adjoining his little room, on 19 September at two o'clock: I renewed an earnest request for his prayers especially for the suffering; I kissed his right hand and he blessed me, placing his wounded hand lightly on my head. Meanwhile he fixed me with his penetrating yet consoling gaze. We parted immediately afterwards, rather hurriedly, as if to hide feelings of joy and deep emotion.

In contrast to my other visits, this time he seemed tired, so much so that he could not say a word; it was as if he wanted to accustom his numerous spiritual children to the long silence which would follow his forthcoming departure from this world.

But yesterday's silence and that of today is an eloquent silence for us, orphans of such a dear father; it speaks to us through his virtues and the example he gave us during his life as a stigmatic priest, a humble son of Francis of Assisi.

His fellow villagers speak of his battles with the spirit of evil along the road which took him from his native village to nearby Piana Romana. I can confirm this as I remember what the Father told me on 23 April 1951 as he was coming out of the friary refectory: 'Modesty apart, no one knows what went on in there at night,' and he clenched his fist; that is all I gathered when I told him I had visited his hut in Piana Romana with my colleagues at that time.

At Pietrelcina, although he was ill, his life had consisted of prayer, sacrifice and the apostolate.

He used to recollect himself in prayer, standing beneath the elm in the field, that elm which is remembered today as the place which witnessed the invisible signs of Christ's passion in his body. And when people tried to distract him, he would say, 'Let me pray.' To those who asked him what was necessary to win eternal life, he would answer, 'An Our Father, a Hail Mary, and a Glory be to the Father, well said and not a hundred of them mumbled carelessly.'

On Sunday, after the celebration of Mass, he did not wish the local women to work even at their crochet, out of respect for the Lord's day.

When he returned from Naples in army uniform during the 1915-1918 war, he tried to arrive home in the evening to put on his friar's habit; once when the neighbours insisted on seeing him in his army uniform, he said 'Happy now that you've seen the clown?'

Father, I wanted to speak to you and your native village, knowing that it would please you. When I remember your village of Pietrelcina, I see you laughing until you cried. I remember that more than once you asked me for detailed news and, last February, when I had come back to celebrate Franciscan Day, you asked me to take greetings to your friends in the village, urging them to be good Christians. And again I remember that you thanked the people who had given you paintings of your birthplace, saying, 'You've given me forty years of life.' Not just forty, Father, but an eternity, to us and to all, with you!

I saw him for the first time, having greatly desired to do so, on 10 May 1945, along with my fellow-student friars on the theological course, on the way back from the feast of Our Lady of Succour in San Severo. He inspired me with great confidence when I heard him talking in such a pleasant and friendly way: 'Is it true,' he asked, 'that they carry all the saints in paradise in the procession at San Severo?' At Matins, seeing us recite the breviary with the lights on, when we could open the shutters and see by the light of day, he remarked, 'It's good to see the young people practising poverty!'

I returned to San Giovanni Rotondo on 19 August 1946 and I stayed for over a month; how much valuable teaching I had from the Father: on perseverance, fervent prayer, deep humility, love of God and neighbour. I will mention only a few episodes among many. As we walked along the corridor I always heard him praying, his rosary in hand; before he went into choir he would make a deep bow and pass the holy water to a lay brother as well; and when a child called him a saint, he answered, 'Now you're blaspheming.' On being asked for advice on how to treat one's neighbour if he failed to observe the monastic silence, he said, 'It doesn't say anywhere that we shouldn't speak, it's just that we should know *how* to speak. What is the use of getting angry? One should say things just as they are and then let others speak as they wish.' When speaking of the interior life and understanding our relationship with God, he encouraged both love and fear, citing St Peter and the traitor Judas to illustrate his point. In his fatherly goodness he gave me a card commemorating my first Mass with this thought from St Paul: 'Let us be other Christs' and he also reminded me of the words: 'Be imitators of me as I am of Christ.'

I was wishing him a good night's sleep after some acute physical suffering (in August 1947), invoking his guardian angel's help, to which he replied, 'What if the angel tells us we have to suffer?'

In bed with his arms crossed, he prayed, 'Lord, may your will be done; make me well, not for my sake but for those poor people.'

In his deep humility this is what he said, 'I should indeed feel daunted when I consider all my sins, my ingratitude, my failures to respond to grace; pray' — and he wept as he said this — 'that I may be converted.'

He was speaking of conversion to the way of holiness.

How can we feel ourselves to be anything but pygmies before a giant like this who, when preaching on humility, described himself as a 'skunk' in the sight of God because of his ingratitude and failure to respond to grace; the glory and beauty of the sun, he used to say, can be dimmed by even the slightest blemish; for him, the sun was God!

Questioned about the perfume that emanated from his person, he answered, 'You want to know too much, lad! To me it's just something natural.'

A conversation I had with him a long time ago, on 15 August 1954, has remained firmly imprinted on my mind and heart.

I was alone with the Father on the terrace from which we could see the town of Foggia illuminated for the feast of the Assumption. I had placed my trembling hand reverently on his shoulder as he sat in a high-backed chair and he said to me, 'Pray and ask others to pray, not that I should suffer or be happy but that the will of God be done in me.'

May those words of the Father provide the programme for our lives so that we can repeat with Jesus in the Garden of Olives, 'Father, your will be done.'

I would like to conclude this brief memoir, beloved Father, by telling you how you showed your emotion to me and some other confrères on one of our frequent visits: 'Father, we have come to see you because we love you very much.' And you thanked us while your pure eyes filled with tears. Now you weep no more; you have wept too much over my sins and those of your children and those of the whole world, which you have helped to redeem by your crucifixion of body and soul.

If you no longer weep because that is now impossible, please be with us still.

Yes, you are with us. I remember what you said to an American soldier who said he would not be able to live without you, 'When you want me, go and kneel before Jesus in the Blessed Sacrament and you will find me there.' We are with you in the presence of the sacramental Christ, at the feet of the Immaculate Virgin, Mother of grace; you loved to venerate her under that title; we are there now and we shall be there forever in heaven.

Chapter 32

Padre Pio's handkerchief

The hospital of Sant'Eugenio in Rome is a huge, sad place, a place of suffering and hope. My younger brother Peppino had been sent there after a bad bout of leukaemia, the last and worst of many attacks he had during his stay in Paris at the Paul Brousse Hospital under the care of Professor Mathé the oncologist who was waging a courageous battle against this incurable blood disease. A few days earlier he had been sent from Paris on his last journey to Italy after Mathé's medical team had said the end was near.

The air journey with my brother Tommaso and me was a heart-breaking homecoming. We seemed to be looking back on a film of our whole childhood, youth and student days. All sorts of memories came to mind and once in a while Peppino would smile as we recalled some of the more amusing episodes of our past life. From time to time he would grow sad and his face betrayed the desperation he felt about his physical condition and the thought of the agonizing days to come.

His stay in Paris in this isolation unit (perhaps it should be called a glass coffin) with a large window onto the corridor and a small telephone to communicate with the outside world, had meant taking continual doses of pills, up to thirty a day, constant blood transfusions, with the ever-renewed search for a tiny area of fresh skin in which to place the needle. From time to time the monotony was broken for the patients' relatives by the crying of children who could no longer endure the enclosed conditions of the 'glass coffins'. Peppino would look at the small photograph of Padre Pio which stood on his bedside table amid a mountain of medicines. It was a sort of secret dialogue. His eyes almost begged Padre Pio to put a stop to the agonizing heartbreak. And when the calm once more returned to the small patients at Paul Brousse Hospital, where their convulsive sobbing stopped as their tears ceased to flow, Peppino would smile happily and take up his rosary again in renewed thanksgiving to the friar of San Giovanni. One morning in February 1984 when he was not yet segregated by the glass coffin, I gave him a handkerchief dipped in blood from Padre Pio's side, telling him he could hold it. His eyes shone with joy as he looked at me, kissed the handkerchief and clasped it between his hands.

A few days later he said to me:

'You know, Tonino, once in a while I cut off a little piece and give it to some patient in this department. If only you knew the surprise and joy I see on the faces of the lucky recipients, just like me!'

'You do well,' I answered, 'but try to please lots of people by cutting less off each time . . .'

'You're stingy even with the relics of the saints!' he smiled.

It was a Sunday morning in November, the first after he had returned from Paris after his horrific experiences at the Paul Brousse Hospital. We were all at my young brother's house after Professor Mathé's team had sent him home. He was stretched out in an armchair when he suddenly got up, staggered out onto the terrace, looked at his son Carlo playing and walked back inside and fell down with a very severe attack. It was his last and most dramatic attack, as it turned out. He was raced in an ambulance to the Hospital of Sant'Eugenio. He was in a coma by then. Nothing could have bettered the expert care he received from Professor Masi, the world-famous haemotologist, or the kind attentions of Professor Pietro Palmisano and Rodolfo Porzio. My younger brother was dying slowly. In a moment of lucidity, he expressed a wish to go to Lacedonia, our home village. We decided to take him there after a brief consultation with the doctors who expected him to die within a few hours.

It was while we were in the ambulance that my brother Tommaso, hoping against hope, slipped Padre Pio's handkerchief into Peppino's breast pocket (he had given it back to me on his return from Paris). We arrived at Lacedonia in the evening. Peppino felt slightly better, he recognized the house and his friends, he became calmer and lived for another three days in his dear Lacedonia where his body now rests. Professor Valerio Consigli, the well-known Roman specialist in integral medicine who had accompanied us and had followed the whole course of the illness, still talks of those three days' lease of life at Lacedonia and says that medically speaking they were quite inexplicable.

Chapter 33

The process of beatification

The process of beatification is a long and difficult one. Decades go by before a servant of God, considered saintly on account of the virtues he or she has practised and the miracles attributed to him or her in life or after death, can be venerated by the Church as a 'blessed'. The process of beatification now in force dates back from two decrees of Pope Urban VIII issued in 1625 and 1634 which entrust the whole matter to the Sacred Congregation of Rites (now the Sacred Congregation for the Causes of the Saints).

It is for the bishop of the diocese to which the future saint belongs, to open the inquiry into the virtues of a servant of God, acquiring documents, testimonies and any other material which may further the cause. Once it has been prepared, the documentation is submitted to the Sacred Congregation for the Causes of the Saints which makes its judgement according to very strict criteria. If this is favourable, the process proper is begun which concludes with the beatification of the servant of God.

At least two miracles are necessary before the cause can proceed to the next stage where a panel of judges makes a more thorough investigation of the virtues of the candidate for beatification, carefully inquiring into the whole life. At these sessions the participants reserve judgement and the strictest criteria are observed and, as in actual beatification hearings, the pope sometimes participates in the proceedings. And it is the pope himself who makes two judgements: one on the conduct and 'heroic virtues' practised (and from that point the servant of God is called 'venerable'), the other on the miracles which must be documented and declared such in default of any scientific explanation of the extraordinary phenomenon. But what does the beatification consist of? It means that a servant of God who has died in the odour of sanctity may be publicly venerated. So people are in fact beatified at the wish of the public, according to popular belief. Evidence of Padre Pio's heroic virtues can be found in such amazing supernatural phenomena as his bilocation, his perfume, the stigmata and many miracles, all of which have led people to consider him a saint.

The day after Padre Pio's death, a powerful car stopped in the little square in front of the friary. Two men got out, one in secular clothes, the other in a cassock. The car left again after several hours, taking two large suitcases of documents and personal effects. That moment probably marked the beginning of the long path which will raise Padre Pio to the altars. But let us review step by step this path which hundreds of thousands of the faithful are following with such deep interest and even anxiety as they await the moment when the friar sent by God may be venerated at the altar.

On 4 November 1969, little more than a year after his death, Father Bernardino da Siena, postulator of the Capuchins, initiated Padre Pio's process of beatification by making a preliminary request concerning the friar to the diocesan bishop, Monsignor Vailati.

On 16 January 1973, the Archbishop of Manfredonia, Monsignor Vailati, having examined the request and acquired the necessary documentation, approached the Sacred Congregation for the Causes of the Saints in Rome in order to obtain permission to introduce the cause of beatification.

On 29 November 1982, Pope John Paul II gave formal permission (eagerly awaited by the faithful) for the opening of the so-called judicial inquiry into the life and virtues (which means the miracles) of Padre Pio. Here is the text of the decree signed by Cardinal Pietro Palazzini:

'In view of the constantly increasing reputation for holiness of the life, virtues and miracles of the servant of God Pio da Pietrelcina (in the civil state Francesco Forgione), professed priest of the Order of Friars Minor (Capuchins), born on 25 May 1887 and deceased 23 September 1968, His Lordship the Right Reverend Antonio Cunial, Apostolic Administrator of Manfredonia, acceding to the request of the Postulator and the desire of many of the faithful, considers it just and right in the service of religion to ask the Holy See *"Sanctitas clarior"* to open or introduce the cause of beatification of the aforesaid servant of God and to institute the judicial inquiry in the diocese of Manfredonia.'

The Sacred Congregation for the Causes of the Saints, having diligently weighed the evidence submitted, on which the cause seems to rest as on legitimate and solid foundations, issued the following decree at the ordinary session on 23 October 1982:

'His Lordship the Right Reverend Valentino Vailati is hereby permitted to proceed to issue the decree for the canonical introduction of the cause of beatification of the servant of God Pio da Pietrelcina (in the civil state Francesco Forgione), professed priest of the Order of Friars Minor (Capuchins) and to institute the judicial inquiry into the life, virtues and miracles of the same, observing all due legal requirements laid down in the aforementioned apostolic decree. Pope John Paul II has been notified of the above matter on 29 November 1982 by the Cardinal Prefect undersigned and His Holiness has ratified and confirmed the response of the Sacred Congregation for the Causes of the Saints.'

23 March 1983 saw the official opening of the judicial inquiry of the cause of beatification of Padre Pio, in the shrine of Our Lady of Grace. After twenty years, this significant stage had been reached but the matter is by no means concluded. Yet the present pope is a friend of Padre Pio. He met him in person in 1947 when the friar foretold his accession to the see of Peter and he went again to San Giovanni as a cardinal and finally as pope, in 1987, he knelt to pray at his tomb. On the other hand, as we have said, processes of beatification in the Church are long and arduous; the evidence brought forward of the 'virtues' of the candidate for sanctity must be good and when one speaks of miracles they must be supported by both faith and science.

But is not the gift of the stigmata perhaps the most eloquent miracle of Padre Pio's life? And the sudden cures from terrible illnesses and the conversion of atheists and the endless stream of people wishing to hear a word from their friar of Gargano — are not these perhaps so many more indications of his sublime closeness to God?

The diocesan judicial inquiry into the life and virtues of

145

Padre Pio in 1988 recorded positive points, favourable to the cause of his beatification and these findings as well as the documentation of any miracles were duly submitted to the Sacred Congregation for the Causes of Saints.

The diocesan judges have yet to complete their investigations into Padre Pio's history before they can submit a finished report of the judicial inquiry to the Tribunal of the Sacred Congregation.

Let us now record the various stages of this process which should lead to the beatification of Padre Pio.

The ecclesiastical Tribunal was set up on 20 March 1983 and began its work on 7 April of the same year with the evidence of the first witness: Father Onorato Marcucci. Between that date and 13 May 1986, the Tribunal held one hundred and eighty-two sessions and heard the testimony of seventy-three witnesses.

The Historical Commission, nominated on 4 June 1983, worked hard to complete the diocesan judicial inquiry which is the first, vital step of the whole process.

However, as well as the laborious and difficult work of the Historical Commission, there is also that of several experts who are making thorough investigations into certain episodes of Padre Pio's life with a view to shedding more light on the friar's spiritual message. All over the world the faithful are eagerly awaiting the day when the Church will beatify Padre Pio.

Chapter 34

Padre Pio and holiness

The further we move in time from Padre Pio's death, the more we become aware of the uniqueness of the events which marked his earthly life, signs of that indefinable but real quality that we call holiness.

Also, since his death we have somewhat lost sight of all the obstacles which even high-ranking members of the clergy saw fit to put in the way of the humble friar of Pietrelcina, how they set up an 'inquisition' to investigate his remarkable activities and sought to hamper or put an end to his religious practices and ministry. His most remarkable achievement was to create the present-day San Giovanni Rotondo out of nothing, building not only an important centre of spirituality but also a huge hospital complex, holiness which ministers to so many sufferers – and all this in a society which is increasingly indifferent to spiritual values, even in less privileged circles.

There is an unchanging, though unfortunately not increasing, respect and devotion of multitudes of great and small alike to Padre Pio's memory and pilgrims continue to flow to San Giovanni Rotondo throughout the year; and it was surely Padre Pio who renewed their devotion to the mystery of the Mass as a precious means of communion with God.

However, it would be unfair not to mention the support the holy Capuchin also received from high-ranking clergy in his movement of religious renewal; among these were the popes of the last few decades who recognized his worth and were able to look beyond both his rough exterior and the controversy surrounding him and see a religious life which was profound and authentic.

The word 'mystery' has been widely used when people have wondered how it was possible to build a hospital complex of the size of the House for the Relief of Suffering which required enormous funds, most of them coming from overseas.

How did the House obtain such widespread publicity?

Something happened in 1924 which may throw some light on the question. It was then, during the early years of the Capuchin's apostolate, that Padre Pio was in a position to 'prove' his mysterious powers to Mary Pyle, the American Protestant heiress, by telling her that he had foreseen the details of her visit and the conversion which would be its outcome; and it was through her that there came an enormous influx of financial aid.

There is a further sign of Padre Pio's charismatic powers in his spontaneous and informal approach to his penitents most of whom were from the more humble social classes and were given to deep religious devotion. This approach was based on the simplicity which runs through the whole history of sainthood and not, as has been wrongly supposed, on a desire to distress or humiliate his penitents. Nor was it pride on the part of the friar. And, again, how could anyone deny that suffering and mortification were fundamental components of the friar's personality, as is evident from the appearance of the stigmata?

Sancta simplicitas, holy simplicity, has been, after all, the motto of the greatest saints, of whom theological aptitude has not always been required, starting, if you will, with Francis of Assisi himself. It is the works performed which count and as far as Padre Pio is concerned these are prodigious, both in the sense of material buildings and in the spiritual sense of the winning of so many souls for the Church of God.

148

Part 2

TESTIMONIES

What they said about him

Hundreds of thousands of people have been able to visit the House for the Relief of Suffering. Although it is a place of pain and suffering, it represents for all who visit it the loftiest and most outstanding monument that charity could have raised through the work of Padre Pio.

So many prelates of the Church, politicians, personalities in the world of culture, entertainment, arts and sciences have written about his work and its originator, Padre Pio.

Cardinal Giacomo Lercaro, Archbishop of Bologna, a great admirer and supporter of Padre Pio's work, wrote this in 1960 on the occasion of the friar's fiftieth anniversary of ordination: 'At San Giovanni Rotondo, in the light of the crucified Saviour, the marks of whose passion are mysteriously present in Padre Pio, there has for a long time been solid teaching on the demands of the Gospel. Hidden at first, this teaching finally took flesh in a House for the Relief of Suffering . . . a wonderful oasis where the Christian spirit permeates all the resources of science and technology in order to bring comfort not only to the body but also to the heart and soul'. And after the death of the friar in 1968, he added: 'He wanted it to be tastefully decorated, a place of beauty open to all the poor free of charge, the same care and loving attention being offered to all alike. Padre Pio has understood the immense dignity of the poor in the Church and he clearly saw the Lord Jesus present in the poor, doubly present in the sick poor. This is the new style of charity. So, following Jesus' example, Padre Pio made himself poor and humble and by his fraternal identification with the poor, he sought to give them on the spiritual plane the succour that riches give the wealthy on the material plane.'

And Raoul Follereau, the apostle of the lepers, the man who had dedicated his life to these poor souls, abandoned by all, said of Padre Pio: 'In this world without faith, ideals

151

or dreams, which holds that human existence is confined to the period between birth and death, the radiant figure of Padre Pio brings us a living message from God. To the poor, the suffering and the persecuted his wounded hands, stretched out in blessing, and his smiling face are the very signs of hope. By virtue of his exceptional mystical communication with the Lord of love, Padre Pio is the greatest benefactor of suffering humanity.'

Among the doctors and men of science who visited the House for the Relief of Suffering were Professor Wangsteen and Professor Gasbarrini. The first said this, 'Just one thing bothers me a lot: that there should be only one Padre Pio in the world.' And Professor Gasbarrini commented, 'With his humility, poverty and charity, Padre Pio has shed the light of Christ on souls near and far as they walk the road of Calvary. The House for the Relief of Suffering is tangible proof of this.'

Padre Pio and his Father Provincial

Father Paolino da Casacalenda, superior of the Friary of San Giovanni Rotondo at the time when the servant of God received the stigmata, has meanwhile become Minister Provincial but he often went to the Gargano district to see Padre Pio and to visit his sister who lived there.

One day he went there during a short period of free time and stayed to lunch with his confrères. At the end of lunch, seeing that Padre Pio had not stayed to talk to him, he called him back and asked for an explanation. 'Reverend Father, you won't be leaving today!' Padre Pio answered him.

When Padre Pio said this, the superior told him that he only just had time to go to his sister's house as the driver was waiting to leave. But when they got there the car did not seem to want to start and they had to wait until next day for a mechanic. When he went back to the friary he met Padre Pio who remarked 'What did I tell you, Reverend Father!'

Padre Pio foretells the future of a fellow friar

At Pietrelcina, Padre Pio's native village, the new church building had been completed and they were trying to think of a way of including Padre Pio in the dedication ceremony without people getting wind of it and thronging to see him in great numbers. But the word went round and Padre Pio was unable to be present at the ceremony. Father Alberto D'Apolito spoke of it one day to Padre Pio and he said he knew the church very well so that he could even tell him the number of steps in front of the door!

The provincial superior, Father Agostino da San Marco in Lamis, once remarked to Padre Pio: 'I would be very happy the day there will be a friary at Pietrelcina!' 'They will open one and you will be the superior!' Padre Pio answered him. 'And on that day I shall be there and, also, in the confessional at San Giovanni.'

Padre Pio in Uruguay

Monsignor Damiani, vicar general of a diocese in Uruguay, wished to die near Padre Pio so as to have the comfort of his presence in his last moments. Padre Pio answered that his mission was not ended and that he would be present at the hour of his death.

Monsignor Barbieri who lived next door to Monsignor Damiani, awoke one night to hear knocks on the door: it was a Capuchin friar who had come to tell him that Monsignor Damiani was dying. The prelate hurried with some other priests to give him the Viaticum and then Monsignor Damiani passed away peacefully. A note was found, written by the dead man, in which he told how Padre Pio had come to see him.

In 1949 Monsignor Barbieri went to San Giovanni Rotondo to visit Padre Pio but above all to clear up his doubts about the strange note. Padre Pio was unwilling to answer the prelate's repeated questions and wanted to hush up the matter. When the Monsignor said, 'I understand,' Padre Pio replied, 'Good! You've understood.'

The monument to Padre Pio

The sculptor Pericle Fazzini was born in Grottammare on the Adriatic coast and died there after having spent all his life in Rome. He was a timid, bashful man who avoided society. He liked to spend his holidays at Grottammare: it was there that he and the architect Eugenio Abruzzini made plans for the square in which the monument to Padre Pio now stands.

Fazzini wrote of himself, 'My statues tend to rise up to the sky . . . there must not be a single line which impedes this upward thrust of each mass; the human figure will be the means by which I will touch the heavens. My figures take shape as if they wanted to free themselves from their own materiality in order to exalt God . . .'

The monument to Padre Pio is Fazzini's masterpiece and sums up his whole philosophy. In it, matter is subjected and shaped so that it tends heavenwards and praises God. The lower part of the monument depicts the temptation of humankind and the devil; the upper part shows the intervention of grace by means of sacraments and mystical gifts. The back shows Padre Pio's bilocation and invites us to liberate ourselves from matter.

As the sculptor wrote in his diary, 'I wish to infuse the human figures in my sculpture with the infinite. I want the soul to be incorporated in plastic form, according to my spiritual condition so that it may be visible to the onlooker. In this way I shall be able to seek and to show my brothers and sisters something which they, too, sense: I am their voice; I gather them up and take them to God.'

The monument to Padre Pio and the square in which it stands were inaugurated on 28 July 1987 in the presence of the Honourable Giulio Andreotti, and numerous religious and political leaders.

Padre Pio: the one called and chosen

The following is the speech made by the Honourable Renato Dell'Andro on 16 April 1989 at San Severo (Foggia) on the occasion of the inauguration of a statue of Padre Pio:

I am extremely happy to be here this evening. And by being here I want to bear witness to our Padre Pio, by showing my own fidelity to the Church and to the ideals for which he lived. I was very pleased to be invited to pay homage above all to the Franciscan Order and to its Capuchin spirituality, and then to remember Padre Pio himself.

We knew Padre Pio and we shall never be able to forget him. Jesus said, 'I know my own and my own know me.' What does it mean, to 'know'? In Greek, 'to know' means an intellectual rapport between one subject and another subject which then becomes an object. In the Hebrew language 'to know' has a very different and much deeper meaning: it means to have a bond which leads people to entrust themselves, to be faithful to one another. I am sure you know Padre Pio not only because you have seen him or have been to his Mass or even made your confession to him but because you know him because you have so often put your trust in him, because you have begun and ended the day by commending yourselves to his protection; because you have seen his works, his actions; because you have read the wonderful thoughts expressed in his letters; because you have been so familiar with him that he became part of your very selves, the soul of your souls.

That is how you have known him, that is how you have loved him. And why? Certainly because of his spiritual gifts and his teaching but above all, I believe, because in him you see one called of God and chosen by God. His stigmata already pointed to such a call. A call to the service of the Absolute, to the Lord, by means of that particular Franciscan spirituality which is the Capuchin way. Chosen, elect, called. Padre Pio was a man called by God. His very body was marked and this caused him great suffering. It was the price he paid for his call. Not for a moment did he go back on his word, never was he unfaithful to the Church. Even in times of darkness and obscurity. We know about some of those times. And at those times he never for an instant wavered in his fidelity to the Church, the Supreme Pontiff, the bishops and hierarchy, nor in his absolutely literal and punctilious adherence to the Franciscan Rule.

Today we remember Padre Pio but at the same time we recall the seven hundred and eightieth anniversary of St

Francis' profession of vows before Innocent III. And as we pay homage to Padre Pio today we also pay homage to St Francis and all the Franciscan saints who have always lived out their Capuchin spirituality in an exemplary manner. And we salute Padre Pio because we see in him all who have faithfully followed that Rule and served St Francis in humility and obedience. Such values are needed in the world today. We need humility.

This evening Padre Pio is present in this monument which you have set up; it stands aloft in the square to show our world the way back to the values of humility and obedience, to Christian values such as service to humanity and to our brothers and sisters in Christ. As I unveiled this statue I thought to myself: Padre Pio has come back among us. And that is in fact what has happened. He has come back. He could not fail to come back because he has come back into our hearts, because he has inspired our love for Christ, for the Church and for St Francis. He has come back to bless us, to tell us he is close to us, that he shares our joys and sorrows.

I would like to end with a plea to all those who are seeking to promote the cause of Padre Pio's beatification: go on with your good work, but be quick about it so that at last we may have a saint from our own land, one who expresses the soul of our own people. On that day, which I hope is not too distant, all of us will be more strongly bound to the Most High, to the Franciscan Order and to Padre Pio.

The first spiritual daughter

'I met Padre Pio as a very young man and I still have a vivid memory of that meeting.' Giuseppe Gargani, chief of the political secretariat for the Christian Democratic Party, spoke with visible emotion of the friar of San Giovanni. 'The name of Padre Pio was familiar in our house at Morra De Sanctis in the Neapolitan region because an aunt of mine, Mother Maria Gargani was his first spiritual daughter and it was actually through his spiritual help that she was able to found the congregation of the Apostles of the Sacred Heart in Naples.'

156

Sister Maria Gargani wrote an account of her own life in a fifty-page exercise book in which she states with great humility, 'Padre Pio asked me to write the story of my life under obedience so I am doing so.' And she adds that Padre Pio himself once solemnly slapped her on the cheek for making a bad confession. Her diary begins with an account of her life at Morra, formerly known as Irpina: 'I was the last of eight children and grew up in a Catholic family, receiving daily religious instruction especially from grandfather.' Her first communion was a sort of prank because she approached the sacrament a long time before the usual age in those days.

At Avellino where she often went to study, 'on my knees beside my little bed, I used to contemplate the crucifix and weep copiously. I had no help and no comfort; Jesus alone was my companion.'

The first meeting with Padre Pio took place at San Marco La Catola in the province of Foggia where the friar had gone in 1915 during the First World War to take the place of Father Agostino who had left for the front as a military chaplain. Padre Pio once said to her smilingly, 'You're not even capable of sinning properly.' Sister Maria goes on: 'Padre Pio was very good at setting my mind at rest but I was fascinated by the way he seemed to see into my very soul, giving the impression that he knew all about me, all my life from childhood onwards.' When all was ready for the departure for Rome, where Maria Gargani was to become a nun, Padre Pio laughed at her when she commended herself to his prayers in the confessional in case she should die: 'How many journeys you still have to make on this earth!' he replied.

Maria Gargani, together with a teacher from Lacedonia, Lina Ferrante, founded an institute for the good of souls. When she told Padre Pio of the difficult beginnings of the project, he exclaimed, 'Now we are where we ought to be'; on the evening of 21 June 1936 she set up house in a convent in Volturara in the province of Foggia and so began the earthly task of Sister Maria Gargani.

The correspondence between Padre Pio and Sister Maria Gargani began in August 1916 when the new sister wrote a letter to Padre Pio asking him to become her spiritual director. Padre Pio did not answer immediately; he first asked Father

Benedetto's permission which was granted. So on 26 August of the same year Padre Pio sent a letter to Sister Maria Gargani in which he declared himself happy to assume the responsibility of following her along her path to God.

In a letter to her family Sister Maria wrote, 'Padre Pio da Pietrelcina knows the whole story of my life; he was the only priest I wanted to turn to in my times of deep spiritual need.'

Sister Maria's letters have not come down to us, while we have some sixty-seven of Padre Pio's, written between 26 August 1916 and 16 May 1923.

During that period, Sister Maria felt that she should found a religious order. Finally, after several letters written to Padre Pio on the subject, the religious institute which took the name of The Apostles of the Sacred Heart came into being. Padre Pio encouraged her, exclaiming joyfully, 'Now we are where we ought to be! This is the will of God and we must soon go to the bishop. How wonderful! How wonderful!'

The congregation was granted diocesan status in 1945 and pontifical status in 1963.

Sister Maria Gargani died on 23 May 1973 in the odour of sanctity. Her whole life had been marked by the love of God and neighbour.

Many anecdotes testify to the spiritual depth of Sister Maria Gargani. It is enough simply to recall that she left her noble family where she could have lived in luxury, in order to embrace the arduous and tortuous path of the religious life. This is what her nephew the Honourable Giuseppe Gargani had to say of her, 'In our family, Aunt Maria was always outstanding for the gentleness which she showed to all her nephews and nieces. At the sight of her we seemed to be freed from our everyday cares. We often heard her mention Padre Pio and I, who was lucky enough to meet him, can never forget the deep emotion I felt when he foretold something in my life, something which I certainly cannot reveal.'

Here is the account of another of Sister Maria Gargani's nephews, Angelo Gargani, a well-known and respected magistrate in Rome: 'I remember Aunt Maria with great affection and regret. She was the light of our family and her words were always full of kindness. She was always smiling and ready to forgive, she loved the humble and defenceless and she was given to prayer and works of charity. She prayed so much that I once asked her if she prayed while she was eating and she answered smiling that one could pray to the Lord at all times, all through life. Now that there is talk of her possible beatification, I am turning to her in prayer because we can truly count ourselves blessed to be of the same family as my aunt.'

Beniamino Gigli and Padre Pio

Padre Pio's meeting with Beniamino Gigli is another instance of the servant of God's ability to read souls, to see into the hidden depths, acting thus as an instrument of God in order to set souls on the right path again.

When Padre Pio met this illustrious person he came straight to the point and rebuked the famous singer for an extra-marital relationship. From that moment Beniamino Gigli broke off the relationship and kept in close touch with Padre Pio until his death.

Like Lazarus

The power of God and the might of Padre Pio's intercession with the Lord are strikingly illustrated in this amazing story.

A mother had a six-month-old son who was seriously ill and was hoping that he could be cured through Padre Pio's intercession. She prepared for the long journey but the child died.

The poor mother did not lose heart and trusting blindly in Padre Pio, wrapped her little son in some clothes and went to San Giovanni Rotondo. When Padre Pio saw the contents of the suitcase, he went pale and began to weep. Looking up to heaven, he prayed intensely for a few minutes and then asked, 'But what's all the fuss about? Can't you see the baby is asleep?' In fact the baby was sleeping peacefully.

As Doctor Sanguinetti who was present at the time confirms, the baby had been dead for some time before the suitcase was opened.

The blind woman

Signora De Giorgi was born with eyes that lacked pupils, and medical science tells us that it is impossible to see without them.

Well, this lady has been able to see since Padre Pio laid his hands on her eyes!

When she was a child her parents soon realized that there was something wrong with her eyes; famous specialists declared that she had no pupils and therefore would never be able to see.

The time came for the little girl's first communion and the grandmother thought of taking her to Padre Pio.

The little girl was told to ask Padre Pio to pray for her healing but she forgot to do so.

But during her confession Padre Pio had placed his hands on her eyes and made the sign of the cross.

When she went to confession the grandmother asked Padre Pio to pray for the little girl and he answered that she should have faith because Gemma had regained her sight.

At communion also, Padre Pio made the sign of the cross over Gemma's eyes: on the return journey the child told her grandmother that she could see clearly – and famous specialists confirmed this.

Padre Pio and the carabinieri

Padre Pio had always had a soft spot for the *carabinieri*. It was in the early fifties that it became known that the mother of the bandit Nardiello had gone to the friary to see Padre Pio.

It was therefore likely that the son, who was roaming the mountains around San Giovanni, would have come to see his mother. The *carabinieri* at the local station had been informed of this and two of them went to the office where applications were made for confession but found neither Nardiello's name or his mother's so went away again.

A little later, an old woman put herself down for confession: it was the bandit's mother.

The friar in charge of applications told Padre Pio and he replied that he would have informed the *carabinieri* afterwards: 'The bandit is armed to the teeth and as soon as he sees them he's sure to bump them off!'

The meeting between the mother and her bandit son took place in the church square: a few words and a swift hug between mother and son. Then the old lady went off again.

Out of his affection for them, Padre Pio had saved the lives of two *carabinieri*.

The picture in the Ardeatine

The day after the allied troops arrived in Rome, on 4 June 1944, I hurried over to the Fosse Ardeatine. I very much wanted to pray in the old quarry which had become a war memorial. I should add that in those final days of Nazi military occupation, I had been longing for the moment of liberation which would enable me to go into that zone of the city which had become something of a symbol.

The scene which met my eyes was horrific: a sort of Dante's *inferno*.

Our soldiers had gathered there a few hours before me; they had been sent to guard the improvised martyrs' cemetery.

Huge heaps of rubble and unexpected holes in the ground made it difficult for me to thread my way to the largest entrance to the quarry where the Jews had been driven in groups and killed. On huge piles of yellow mud lay the bodies of our three hundred and thirty-five poor brothers, many of them my dear friends for we had fought and believed and endured side by side. Poor dear martyrs with whom I had shared privation, suffering, danger in occupied Rome, all of us fired by the illusive dream of a more just and honourable Italy, none of us suspecting what was to become of our dear country . . .

It was difficult to walk forward and at times one had to

161

go on all fours. I gaped in stupefaction at that *inferno* and I was heartbroken as I thought tenderly of dear Uccio Pisino, Aladino Govoni and so many other unforgettable friends and companions who were barbarously killed because they were 'guilty' as I was 'guilty' – martyrs who thought and acted as I did; but unlike them I was more fortunate and somehow or other I had escaped.

I thought above all of three occasions when I had had unexpected, miraculous escapes without which I too, would have been led inexorably to that place of martyrdom. Three times before the killings that path to death opened up before me and each time a mysterious force mercifully diverted my steps . . . The first time was when I was arrested on 2 January 1944 with four of my friends and incarcerated in the improvised underground prison which had been hollowed out beneath the Widechit Palace. We were subsequently released during those dark and terrible days thanks to the cunning trick of a friend who risked his life by posing as a high official of the Armed forces and he got us out of prison, at which point we all took to our heels under a hail of belated gunfire.

The second time was about a month before the killings when I arrived a few minutes late for a secret meeting near the Church of Sant'Andrea delle Fratte where other friends were arrested. I was warned in time of the danger by an old man who had been appalled to witness the sad arrest a few minutes earlier. He whispered this alarming warning to me: 'Clear off!'

And again, the third time, it was 19 March, five days before the killings, when I had cautiously come out for a brief hour from my hiding-place. I was going to meet friends of mine at their house in the Piazza Barberini. I was hoping to have a meal with them during those days of hunger: it was the feast of St Joseph and we were going to eat something different from the usual piece of black bread we usually had. Coming out of a side street, creeping along the wall, I came to the front door of number 5 Piazza Barberini. I was stopped by the faithful doorman who was standing on the threshold of the front door and said, all in one breath, 'Get out, clear off, they're searching upstairs, two officers from the Gestapo and four Italian policemen from the SS.' A spy had put the police on my trail.

During my visit to the Ardeatine, I shuddered as I thought of those episodes which now flashed through my mind and moved me very deeply. At a certain moment I bent down to pick up a photo of a young friar which was lying at my feet. I thought perhaps it was a priest relative or friend of the unknown martyr out of whose pocket it had fallen. I dusted the little photo and treating it almost as a relic through which I had touched the unknown owner, I placed it reverently in my wallet.

A month later I was lucky enough to be able to go to my home in distant Sicily where my parents were anxiously awaiting me. As my mother embraced me fondly she confided to me that she had often prayed to God for my safety and also asked the prayers of a saint living in Puglia to whom she was devoted; she prayed most fervently every day and often wrote to him. 'You too should be grateful to him, and show your devotion; he's the young friar with the stigmata,' she told me. And she handed me Padre Pio's picture. I went pale. It was the same face as in the small photograph I had picked up from the ground!

APPENDIX

Biographical notes on Padre Pio

25 May 1887

He is born at Pietrelcina in the province of Benevento in southern Italy. His parents were Giuseppa and Orazio Forgione. He was baptized the following day in the Church of Santa Maria degli Angeli in Pietrelcina with the name of Francesco.

6 January 1903

At the age of sixteen he is clothed in the Francescan habit taking the name of Fra Pio, in the Capuchin friary at Morcone also in the province of Benevento.

10 August 1910

He is ordained priest in the chapel of the Archbishop's Palace in Benevento and on 14 August he celebrates his first Mass at Pietrelcina amid great rejoicing on the part of his parents and fellow villagers. Before being ordained priest Padre Pio had attended the school near the Friary of Sant'Elia a Pianisi (Campobasso) and had gone on to study philosophy in 1906 at the Friary of San Marco La Catola (Foggia) and also that of Sant'Elia at Pianisi. In 1907 he began his theological studies at the Friary of Serracapriola (Foggia) and at the house of studies at Montefusco (Avellino).

6 November 1915

He is called up by the army but on account of his poor health he will be sent home again on 16 March 1916 with double broncho-pneumonia.

17 February 1916

Padre Pio goes to Foggia to minister spiritually to a certain Raffaelliano Cerase. It was on that occasion that the father provincial told Padre Pio to stay at the friary. Padre

Pio remained at Foggia until 4 September of that year and was then transferred to San Giovanni Rotondo.

16 May 1917

He accompanies his sister Graziella to Rome where she enters the Bridgettine order and then returns to San Giovanni Rotondo on 23 May.

20 September 1917

He receives the gift of the stigmata, five wounds dripping with blood which will remain the same for fifty years. He had begged the Lord to let these wounds remain invisible; he also tried to hide them but was unsuccessful. Padre Pio's earthly agony begins. Church authorities make him undergo various medical examinations. The friars of the convent are beginning to be accused of 'commercializing Padre Pio's stigmata' and the friar himself is branded as an impostor. On 22 June 1922, following the uproar about the friar of San Giovanni, the Holy Office imposes a series of restrictions on his activities; these range from stopping his correspondence with his spiritual father, Benedetto da San Marco in Lamis, to warning the faithful not to approach Padre Pio, to prohibiting Padre Pio from celebrating in public and corresponding with the faithful.

Between 1924 and 1928 three apostolic visitors are sent to San Giovanni Rotondo: Padre Celestino da Desio, Monsignor Felice Bevilacqua and Monsignor Bruno of the Congregation of the Council.

September 1925

Padre Pio undergoes a surgical operation without anaesthetic at his express wish. Because of the great physical pain, he loses consciousness. It was a hernia in the groin.

3 January 1929

His mother dies and Padre Pio is grief-stricken and weeps for three days and prays stretched out on his bed.

23 May 1931

He is suspended from all forms of ministry except the Mass which he must celebrate alone in the indoor chapel of the friary. When they read to him the decree of the Holy Office Padre Pio raises his eyes heavenwards and exclaims, 'May the Lord's will be done' and, barely holding back his tears, goes off towards the choir of the little church where he remains in prayer until late into the night. Thus begins the saddest period of Padre Pio's life where he lives in complete isolation giving his time to prayer.

14 July 1933

Padre Pio is permitted to hear confessions and to celebrate Mass in public. He begins to smile after his two years of segregation. From that moment Padre Pio begins to follow a routine which will continue until his death. He rises very early, celebrates a Mass that lasts about two hours, hears confessions until midday, goes back to church for evening prayer, hears more confessions and spends the rest of the time in his cell praying.

9 January 1940

In Padre Pio's cell is born the idea of building the House for the Relief of Suffering. On that cold evening with Padre Pio there were Doctor Guglielmo Sanguinetti, Doctor Mario Sanvico and Doctor Carlo Kiswaday.

19 May 1947

Construction work on the House for the Relief of Suffering begins.

7 October 1947

His father also dies. Padre Pio watches with him most lovingly and when he dies exclaims, 'Papa, my Papa! . . .'

5 May 1956

Inauguration of the House for the Relief of Suffering in the presence of Cardinal Giacomo Lercaro. On 2 July the first stone is laid for the new Church of Santa Maria delle Grazie (Our Lady of Grace) next to the old church.

25 April 1959

Padre Pio falls seriously ill; they fear for his life. He is taken to the House for the Relief of Suffering and stays there scarcely three days before returning suddenly to his friary. He recovers on 6 August while a statue of Our Lady of Fatima is landing by helicopter at San Giovanni Rotondo.

30 June 1960
The visit of Monsignor Maccari begins with new and more severe restrictions for Padre Pio. There is much press coverage of the event. There is talk of a transfer to Spain. Finally on 30 January 1964 Cardinal Ottaviani writes to inform Padre Pio that he may pursue his ministry with absolute liberty. In 1967 Paul VI sends the Bishop of Benevento, Monsignor Raffaele Calabria, to San Giovanni Rotondo.

20 September 1968
Solemn celebrations of the fiftieth anniversary of Padre Pio's stigmata.

21 September 1968
International convention of prayer groups.

22 September 1968
He celebrates his last Holy Mass.

23 September 1968
He dies at 2.30 a.m.

4 November 1969
Preliminary preparations for the cause of beatification and canonization are begun.

16 January 1973
Monsignor Valentino Vailati, Archbishop of Manfredonia, submits to the Sacred Congregation for the Causes of the Saints all the required documentation to obtain the *nihil obstat* for the introduction of the cause of beatification.

3 March 1980
The same Archbishop submits to the above-mentioned Congregation further documentation to obtain the desired *nihil obstat*.

20 March 1983

Official opening of the judicial inquiry into the life and virtues of the servant of God, Padre Pio da Pietrelcina.

The popes of Padre Pio

Leo XIII (1878–1903)

When Padre Pio was born in 1887, Leo XIII was pope. He is remembered as the pope of the rosary and of *Rerum Novarum*. Leo XIII and Padre Pio: two apostles of the rosary, two devotees of Mary, two great benefactors of the sick and the suffering.

St Pius X (1903–1914)

After the death of Leo XIII, Giuseppe Sarto, Patriarch of Venice, was elected pope, taking the name of Pius X. He is remembered for his work of reform in the Church and for his famous encyclical *Pascendi* of 1907. Padre Pio very much loved this pope who had offered himself as a victim to God possibly to avert the First World War.

Benedict XV (1914–1922)

Cardinal Giacomo Della Chiesa succeeded Pius X, taking the name of Benedict XV. During this period the name of Padre Pio became known all over the world because he had received the gift of the stigmata. The pope recognized in Padre Pio 'an extraordinary man, of the sort whom God sends on earth from time to time to convert humanity.'

Pius XI (1922–1939)

On 6 February 1922, Achille Ratti, Archbishop of Milan, was elected pope, taking the name of Pius XI. During his pontificate Padre Pio was subjected to very painful trials. These were the years of segregation and feared transfer. The supernatural character of the phenomena attributed to Padre Pio was not recognized, he was forbidden to celebrate in public, to hear confessions and to answer letters addressed to him. All this went on for ten years: Padre Pio endured it with obedience and resignation. In 1933 Pius XI permitted Padre Pio to resume his priestly ministry.

172

Pius XII (1939–1958)

Cardinal Eugenio Pacelli was elected pope on 2 March 1939 taking the name of Pius XII. This pope, having thoroughly understood the spirit of Padre Pio, promoted his work and gave full support to his priestly ministry and his projects in aid of the suffering. During this period the prayer groups came into being and work was started on the House for the Relief of Suffering. This pope showed endless goodwill towards Padre Pio. Pius XII died at Castelgandolfo on 9 October 1958.

John XXIII (1958–1963)

On 28 October 1958, Angelo Roncalli was elected pope, taking the name of John XXIII. During his pontificate Padre Pio's work experienced a fresh impulse but slander and calumny started all over again. Pope John made up his mind completely about Padre Pio after a conversation with Monsignor Andrea Cesarano, Archbishop of Manfredonia. John XXIII, the good pope, died on 3 June 1963.

Paul VI (1963–1978)

On 21 June 1963 Giovanni Battista Montini, Archbishop of Milan, was elected pope, taking the name of Paul VI. He had been informed of Padre Pio's work since 1954 and he sought to develop and expand the prayer groups, at the same time restoring full freedom to Padre Pio. Paul VI died on 6 August 1978.

John Paul I (26 August-28 September 1978)

Albino Luciani, Patriarch of Venice, was elected pope on 26 August 1978 and chose the name of John Paul I. His pontificate was cut short by his death on 28 September 1978.

John Paul II (16 October 1978-)

Amid general amazement on 16 October 1978 a Polish cardinal was elected pope. He took the name of John Paul II. He had met Padre Pio during a visit to San Giovanni Rotondo in 1947. The memory of Padre Pio will remain with him all his life. On 1 November 1974, while still Archbishop of Cracow, he went to San Giovanni Rotondo to commemorate the

173

twenty-eighth anniversary of his ordination to the priesthood. He returned there as pope in May 1987 and prayed at the tomb of Padre Pio.

TERESA NEUMANN

Paola Giovetti

For decades the story of the stigmatist of Konnersreuth inflamed the passions of thousands of Germans and was the centre of violent discussions.

With accuracy and verve Paola Giovetti here recounts Teresa Neumann's life. The present work is the result of years of rigorous research. From 1926 when the stigmas began to appear till her death in 1962, Teresa neither ate nor drank anything, so much so that during the last War the Nazis took back her ration card on the pretext that she did not need food!

This very ordinary farm girl not once lamented about the excruciating pain and sufferings she underwent; instead she always cheerfully offered her sufferings for the salvation of humanity.

Despite the fact that she was the subject of a variety of praeternatural happenings, she led a simple life like the rest of her townspeople. Her life is a call and a reminder to all to come closer to Christ in the Eucharist and it will certainly help us to understand better the meaning of suffering in human life.

144 pages   ISBN 085439 3463   £6.95

THE CHEERFUL GIVER
Margaret Sinclair

by Felicity O'Brien

Margaret Ann Sinclair was born on 29th March 1900, in Edinburgh. For twenty-three years she lived an ordinary family life reaching out to people with her constant serenity and cheerfulness. She joined the Poor Clares in 1923, and died of tuberculosis at the age of twenty-five.

Margaret's holiness was already manifest among her contemporaries. She is an outstanding example and source of inspiration for Christians today.

FELICITY O'BRIEN is a freelance writer. For a number of years she worked with the Catholic weekly, The Universe. From there she moved on to take charge of the publications department of the Independent Broadcasting Authority. She lives in Kent.

ISBN 085439 310 2   89 pages   £4.25

NO GREATER LOVE

Damien apostle of the lepers

by John Milsome

This is the story of a man – Joseph de Veuster, better known as Father Damien, "the hero of Molokai" – who devoted his life to the welfare of the lepers on the island of Molokai, in the Pacific Ocean. The conditions on the island were daunting. The lepers lived in squalor and misery. Being a foreigner he was not at once welcomed by the lepers. His "ragged honesty, generosity and mirth" however, won them over as friends. What is Damien's relevance for us today? Basically three things: fidelity to one's calling, dedication to a worthy cause and compassion for the underprivileged and outcasts of the society.

Robert Louis Stevenson wrote of Damien: "It was his part, by one striking act of martyrdom, to direct all men's eyes on this distressful country. At a blow and with the price of his life, he made the place illustrious and public... If ever any man brought reforms and died to bring them, it was he." This is the challenge unfolded in the pages of *No Greater Love*.

JOHN MILSOME was born in Pinner, Middlesex. He trained as a teacher and his main interest outside teaching was his writing career. The completion of No Greater Love *was sealed with his premature death.*

ISBN 085439 308 0   105 pages   £5.25

THROUGH THE EYE OF A NEEDLE

Frédéric Ozanam

by Austin Fagan

Child of the 19th century, Frédéric Ozanam is an extraordinarily relevant figure for our time.
Exceptionally gifted with a precocious intelligence and a prophetic intuition, he had at a very early age, the foreboding of the tearings of our world and the cleavage between the strong and the weak, the rich and the poor.
Dr Austin Fagan has accurately described the various aspects of the rich personality of the principal founder of the Society of St Vincent de Paul: delicacy of family feelings, sense of friendship, spiritual radiance, professional conscientiousness, dedication to public affairs. Frédéric's was a truly prophetic voice that can still inspire many to speak out and act with the poor and the underprivileged of society today.

DR AUSTIN FAGAN, a graduate of Manchester University, was awarded a M Litt for his thesis entitled The political and social ideas of Antoine-Frédéric Ozanam (1813-53) and their relationship to the movement of ideas in his time. *In 1988 he was elected President of Manchester SVP Central Council and also became a Vice-President of the National Council.*

ISBN 085439 313 7   212 pages   £5.95

NOT PEACE BUT A SWORD

John Henry Newman

by Felicity O'Brien

'He followed the truth wherever it led him'. This description by Cardinal Newman of someone who greatly influenced him in his early life may be applied to Newman himself. At the age of 15 he underwent a conversion experience. From then on he pursued the truth 'wherever it led him'. The autor, delving into a large collection of letters, sermons, articles and books by Newman, portrays him as a passionate seeker of holiness and a champion of truth. In times when indifference can masquerade as tolerance, and steadfast loyalty to a creed can degenerate into religious fanaticism, this book cuts finely through the mists of both apathy and bigotry, and offers to the reader the companionship of an unshakable believer.

FELICITY O'BRIEN is a freelance writer. For a number of years she worked with the Catholic weekly, The Universe. From there she moved on to take charge of the publications department of the Independent Broadcasting Authority. She lives in Kent.

ISBN 085439 327 7   185 pages   £5.95

MAN OF THE BEATITUDES
Pier Giorgio Frassati
by Luciana Frassati

"The man of the eight beatitudes" – this is how John Paul II described Pier Giorgio Frassati, otherwise known to his friends as "Robespierre" or "The Terrible". Born in Turin in 1901, the only son of Alfredo Frassati – founder of the prestigious Italian newspaper, *La Stampa* – Pier Giorgio "represented the pure, happy, fine Christian youth interested in social problems, who had the Church and its fate at heart" (Karl Rahner). A magnificent athlete and gifted with exuberant high spirits and humour, Pier Giorgio bore a courageous witness of Christian faith and charity to others, especially towards the very poor and suffering. A fatal illness cut short Pier Giorgio's life at the premature age of 24. Young men and women will find in Pier Giorgio an inspiring Christian model in facing the challenges of modern times.

LUCIANA FRASSATI, Pier Giorgio's sister, was born in 1902 in Pollone, Italy. She graduated with honours in jurisprudence in 1923. Married to a Polish diplomat, and the mother of six children, she devoted much time and her literary skill in publishing books about the life and personality of her brother Pier Giorgio.

ISBN 085439 286 6   187 pages   £5.95